SEP _ 2015

791.4365 BRODERICK
Brod
Real
Holly

D0922925

WITHDRAWN

REAL WAR VS. REEL WAR

Film and History
Series Editor: Cynthia J. Miller

REAL WAR VS. REEL WAR

Veterans, Hollywood, and WWII

Suzanne Broderick

ROWMAN & LITTLEFIELD
Lanham • Boulder • New York • London

Alameda Free Library
1550 Oak Street
Alameda, CA 94501

Published by Rowman & Littlefield
A wholly owned subsidiary of The Rowman & Littlefield Publishing Group, Inc.
4501 Forbes Boulevard, Suite 200, Lanham, Maryland 20706
www.rowman.com

Unit A, Whitacre Mews, 26-34 Stannary Street, London SE11 4AB

Copyright © 2015 by Rowman & Littlefield

All rights reserved. No part of this book may be reproduced in any form or by any electronic or mechanical means, including information storage and retrieval systems, without written permission from the publisher, except by a reviewer who may quote passages in a review.

British Library Cataloguing in Publication Information Available

Library of Congress Cataloging-in-Publication Data

Broderick, Suzanne, 1948–
Real war vs. reel war : veterans, Hollywood, and WWII / Suzanne Broderick.
pages cm — (Film and history)
Includes bibliographical references and index.
Includes filmography.
ISBN 978-1-4422-4555-6 (hardback : alk. paper) — ISBN 978-1-4422-4556-3 (ebook) 1. World War, 1939–1945—Motion pictures and the war. 2. War films—United States—History and criticism. 3. World War, 1939-1945—Personal narratives, American. 4. Motion pictures and history. 5. Soldiers in motion pictures. 6. Prisoners of war in motion pictures. I. Title.
D743.23.B753 2015
791.43'6584054—dc23
2014036218

∞™ The paper used in this publication meets the minimum requirements of American National Standard for Information Sciences Permanence of Paper for Printed Library Materials, ANSI/NISO Z39.48-1992.

Printed in the United States of America

To all WWII veterans,
especially my father, James Broderick Jr., U.S. Navy,
and my uncle, Harry Miller, U.S. Army

CONTENTS

INTRODUCTION

This book is built on the idea that Hollywood films deserve a role in the study of history: that these films are valuable in depicting the details and capturing the spirit of the past, and are capable of conveying important truths about it. Because they are intended as entertainment, however, these films can also be problematic: distorting historical details, or altering the course of events, for the sake of a more engrossing story. Hollywood's depictions of World War II reflect both these truths.

The chapters that follow look at the historical accuracy of a number of films about the Second World War through the eyes of war veterans. In comparing their own real-life war experiences with the ones portrayed on the screen, these men and women attempt to answer the question, "Can Hollywood films such as *Battleground* (1949), *Guadalcanal Diary* (1943), *Sands of Iwo Jima* (1949), *Back to Bataan* (1945), *Twelve O'Clock High* (1949), *Memphis Belle* (1944 and 1990), *The Great Escape* (1963), *Wing and a Prayer* (1944), and *Windtalkers* (2002) be considered valid historical narratives?" Seven different veterans watched at least one Hollywood war film and then commented on different aspects of the movies' realism. These veterans represent widely varied war experiences: they include two U.S. Army infantrymen—one from the European Theater and another from the Pacific Theater—and three pilots; the captain of a B-17 in the Eighth Air Force; a U.S. Navy pilot stationed on aircraft carriers in the Pacific; and another Eighth Air Force pilot who was shot down and held as a prisoner of war. Also included is a Navajo code talker who, as a very young Marine, took part in the Battle of Iwo Jima, and two women who were "home front veterans" and worked as real-life versions of "Rosie the Riveter." The veterans' wartime memories, even after more than fifty years, were still vivid, and their recall of details was remarkable. Their war experiences, both in combat and at home, have not been easily forgotten or altered by memory. With their many recollections in mind, these veterans closely watched Hollywood's dramatizations of war for accuracies as well as inaccuracies.

The first interviewee, Harry Miller, is a former infantryman who fought in the Battle of the Bulge—Germany's last major ground offensive—in December 1944. He comments, in chapter 2, on the 1949 film *Battleground* and its claims of authenticity in re-creating that strategic battle. He agrees that both the look ("same snow") and especially the sounds of *Battleground* are highly realistic. He also corroborates several details featured in the film that only a veteran of the battle would recognize: the "buddy system" among the soldiers, the mail delivery, and even the knife that star Van Johnson wears strapped to his pant leg.

In chapter 3 the focus moves to the war in the Pacific, as remembered by Jim Hoisington, a Navy pilot who flew from aircraft carriers in the Pacific. His comments on Hollywood's version of his role in the war, after viewing *Wing and a Prayer*, are supplemented by remembrances from his memoirs and a letter to the author. He concludes that *Wing and a Prayer*'s depiction of pilots' lives on board "Carrier X" accurately reproduces his own World War II living conditions on the carriers *Enterprise*, *Intrepid*, and *Hancock*.

In chapter 4, Jim Oberman, a former member of the Eighth Air Force, recalls the thirty-five missions he flew over Europe as the pilot of a B-17 bomber and compares his experiences with those portrayed in the 1944 documentary and 1990 docudrama versions of *Memphis Belle* and *Twelve O'Clock High*. Although Oberman admires the earlier version of *Memphis Belle* and also praises parts of the latter, he states that *Twelve O'Clock High* is *the* movie about the Eighth Air Force, primarily because it is based on an actual episode from the Eighth's bombing campaign against Nazi Germany.

Chapter 5 moves the focus back to the South Pacific, where the war and Hollywood are discussed by Lynn Simpson, a veteran of thirty months in combat zones and numerous heated battles. Simpson recounts his many combat experiences and compares them to the Pacific war depicted in *Guadalcanal Diary, Back to Bataan,* and *Sands of Iwo Jima*. In general, he approves of much of the wartime history that these films convey and is especially impressed with the historical accuracy of *Sands of Iwo Jima*.

Ernest Thorp was not able to complete his thirty-five-mission tour as the copilot of an Eighth Air Force bomber; he was shot down on his eighteenth mission and spent the rest of the war in a prisoner-of-war camp in Germany. In chapter 6, Thorp discusses his incarceration in Stalag Luft III, where earlier hundreds of prisoners dug three cleverly concealed escape tunnels, and seventy-six broke out one night in 1944. Thorp testifies to the accuracy of Hollywood's all-star, big-budget dramatization of those events in *The Great Escape*, finding the film factual down to the tiniest (almost unbelievable) details.

Chapter 7 focuses on Thomas Begay, a Navajo and former U.S. Marine "code talker" and his comments on *Windtalkers*, a heavily fictionalized film in which the code talkers of the title—who used their native language as a virtually unbreakable code for conveying tactical information—actually play supporting roles behind the very non-Navajo Marine sergeant played by Nicolas Cage. When asked about the historical accuracy of this Hollywood production, Begay gave a vehement thumbs down.

Finally, two women who toiled on the home front, Marge Mehlberg and Lucille Broderick, watched such films as *Since You Went Away*, *Tender Comrade*, *Swing Shift*, and the documentary *The Life and Times of Rosie the Riveter*. In chapter 8 the women relate their varied wartime experiences, providing a picture of home-front life during war, and commenting on the picture created by the films.

These veterans of the battlefield and the home front do not profess to be speaking for all of the Second World War generation, nor do they pretend to be film scholars or experts on military history; they are simply relating their own personal experiences and commenting on how Hollywood interpreted these experiences. That said, with their invaluable assistance, this study confirms that Hollywood *can* successfully record history accurately.

Several World War II films have been produced in this and the past decade. The first generation of these films—produced during and immediately after the war (1942–1962), and often shaped by the cast and crew's own wartime experiences—was followed by a second generation dominated by epic re-creations of specific engagements: *The Longest Day* (1962), *The Battle of the Bulge* (1965), *Tora! Tora! Tora!* (1970), *Mid-*

way (1976), and *A Bridge Too Far* (1978). Films about World War II declined in the late 1970s and 1980s as Vietnam-era films like *Apocalypse Now* (1979) and contemporary military dramas like *Top Gun* (1985) took center stage, but beginning with Steven Spielberg's *Saving Private Ryan* (1998) there has been a newfound interest in depicting the battles of 1939–1945 onscreen. The Second World War has been "discovered" by a younger generation of American filmmakers who have produced, in the first decade of the twenty-first century alone, films such as *U-571* (2000), *Pearl Harbor* (2001), *Inglourious Basterds* (2009), *Monuments Men* (2014), and *Fury* (2014). Films such as these do not claim accuracy nor, for the most part, do they achieve it. They are produced by filmmakers several generations removed from the war—who possess no firsthand wartime memories of their own—and made for audiences in which World War II veterans are a dwindling minority. The difference this can make is apparent in the contrast between Harry Miller's respect for the accuracy of *Battleground* (1949) and code talker Thomas Begay's derisive dismissal of the Hollywood fantasy of *Windtalkers* (2002).

The comments of World War II veterans provides an invaluable perspective on Hollywood's depictions of the war. Before looking at World War II film "history," however, we should first consider the relationship between film and history in general. Not long ago, most historians would have railed against the suggestion that the field of history could have any use for Hollywood films, but that view is slowly changing. The book begins, then, with a look at how a group of pioneering scholars made a case for the relevance of film to the study of history, paving the way for history teachers—and history students—of all levels to integrate film into their explorations of the past.

1

HOLLYWOOD, HISTORY, AND THE HISTORIAN

On January 4, 1997, the American Historical Association met in New York City. At this meeting, a panel discussion—now known as the "Oliver Stone Session"—took place in a room full of interested historians. The panel, convened to discuss Stone's film *Nixon* (1995), consisted of respected historian Arthur M. Schlesinger Jr., history maker George McGovern, and filmmaker Oliver Stone. One member of the audience, Peter C. Rollins, remembers that "they [the historians] hung on Stone's every word" as Stone spoke about his understanding of history, and his role as not merely a filmmaker, but as a "popular historian."[1] Many would disagree with Stone's self-ascribed role, drawing a much sharper distinction between those who study and write history and those who dramatize it. This uneasy association has been at issue since the last decade of film's first complete century. Before the 1990s, historians generally believed that the two fields were mutually exclusive: that no legitimate reason existed for filmmakers to become involved in history, nor was there any reason for historians to become involved in filmmakers' art. Even today, questions persist: How do we better understand the relationship between the two fields? Does film have any legitimate link to history? What manner of history does film convey?

From its very beginnings, film has, to borrow a phrase from noted historian and film scholar Robert Rosenstone, "revisioned history." Moviemakers, in other words, have regularly interpreted historical events to suit their own commercial, artistic, and ideological purposes, and thereby influenced viewers' perceptions of the past. To early American movie-goers, the Civil War and D. W. Griffith's film *Birth of a Nation* (1915) were one and the same—indivisible. In *Battleship Potemkin* (1925), Sergei Eisenstein brought the spirit of the Russian Revolution to life on the screen for millions of Soviets to witness and applaud. Director Abel Gance, employing innovative film techniques, made film history with the biographical epic *Napoleon* (1927). Although these three films have come to be accepted as classics, most movies dealing with historical subject matter have been considered far less favorably by the majority of historians, and seen as negligible contributions to history, if not downright travesties of it. Many historians saw popular film—with its emphasis on entertainment and frequent reliance on formula—as incompatible with accurate depictions of the past. History and filmmaking were, if not adversaries, fundamentally different enterprises with nothing to say to each other. After a century of filmmaking, however, those views began to change. Historians gradually accepted that dramatic films not only could be used to interest the public in the true historical stories that inspired them, but also could be viewed and studied as artifacts of the eras in which they were produced and released, thus providing a reflection of an earlier America. Many respected historians have studied the films of various historical periods and concluded that movies serve as excellent reflectors of the conditions, the attitudes, and the social and political climate of their day.

Today, "Hollywood history" has become too pervasive to be ignored. Historians frequently debate the merits of filmmakers' interpretations of history, along with the larger question of whether or not film is even an appropriate medium for the conveyance of historical subject matter. Several works appeared in the 1970s that heralded this change in attitude toward film's role in history. In 1971, Andrew Bergman published *We're in the Money*, a book concerned with the Great Depression in the United States; Bergman, however, did not take a traditional historian's approach to the Depression. Instead, he chose to view it as seen from "the Bijous, the Gems, and the Orpheums," the movie theaters found in the small towns and large cities across America. Bergman discussed the ways in which Hollywood dealt with the Depression, how the Depression affected the movies themselves, and what the theaters showed every week to those Americans who chose to exchange their few precious coins for an afternoon's or evening's worth of Hollywood-style entertainment.

Bergman demonstrated that we can learn a great deal about Depression-era America by studying the films that Americans of this period paid to see. Like many adolescents of that generation who were forced into early adulthood by economic hardship, a fledgling Hollywood found itself confronted with a Herculean task: to entertain a nation that had little to smile or laugh about, and unify audiences through their shared experiences of motion picture comedy, drama, and suspense, moderating the bitter class divisions that also marked the era. This strategy worked well, according to Bergman: "During the most abysmal days of the early thirties . . . movie attendance still averaged an astonishing sixty to seventy-five million persons per week."[2] The movies became vital to Americans; Hollywood's films played an essential role in enabling the country to survive those lean, sad years. Films, as Bergman observes, were not just luxuries, but had become "as necessary as any other daily commodity."[3]

According to Bergman, Hollywood's mission during the Depression was to support traditional American belief in the possibility of individual success and the benevolence of the federal government. Hollywood was to keep alive the myth of a mobile and classless society by focusing on the endless possibilities for individual success, by turning social evil into personal evil, and by fashioning the New Deal into a veritable leading man.[4]

The overriding theme of Bergman's work is summed up by this tune, sung by Ginger Rogers in *Gold Diggers of 1933*:

> We're in the money,
> We're in the money,
> We've got a lot of what it takes to get along.
> We never see a headline
> About a breadline
> Today.[5]

Hollywood filmmakers hoped that making light of America's economic woes would serve as a "safety valve" for the tensions of the day, as well as uplift moviegoers. The popularity of this film, and others like it, proved them correct.

Bergman's argument that films could serve as legitimate documents for historical study opened the door for other scholars in the field. In 1975, Robert Sklar published *Movie-Made America*, an overview of the social history of Hollywood filmmaking. With this text, film's complex relationship with society now had a history of its own, worthy of study.

Another of the earliest books on the subject of film and history to be taken seriously by historians was *American History/American Film*. Published in 1979, this collection of essays features a foreword by Arthur M. Schlesinger Jr., in which the renowned historian acknowledges that scholars involved in the study of history have traditionally held a low opinion of American films:

> Historians are a conservative lot. Movies have had status problems ever since they emerged three quarters of a century ago as dubious entertainment purveyed by immigrant hustlers to a working-class clientele in storefront holes-in-the-wall scattered through the poorer sections of the industrial city.[6]

For Schlesinger, American films represented the "unstable merger of commerce and art."[7] Even so, he believed that films merit some attention from historians: "The earliest filmmakers saw their invention as a record-keeping device, a modern way of recording real events."[8]

However, these "earliest filmmakers"—documentarians, those noble and enlightened recorders of history—were quickly outnumbered in the film industry by not-so-noble filmmakers who were more interested in profiting than chronicling. They prospered by providing the masses with affordable and desirable entertainment with little concern for historical accuracy. However, as Jack Shadoian argues, even these "entertainment for profit only" films can be of use to the historian: "All films are ultimately about something that interests and/or bothers the culture they grew out of."[9]

Hollywood as Historian, a major early work in this field, was published in 1983. In the introduction to this collection, editor Peter C. Rollins affirms that "Hollywood's myth and symbols are permanent features of America's historical consciousness"[10] and contends that "Hollywood has often been the unwitting recorder of national moods. In recent years Hollywood has used musicals, westerns, gangsters, and other escapist fares of the 1930s to decode messages about the Depression generation's hopes and fears."[11] Rollins also observes that Hollywood was often not satisfied with merely passively recording America's collective sentiments; it also attempted to influence history "by turning out films consciously designed to change attitudes towards matters of social or political importance."[12] Rollins, along with the contributors to *Hollywood as Historian*, discussed how individual films provide information on the country's attitude toward racism, sexism, the Cold War, the Red Scare, and so on. [13]

That same year another volume, Biskind's *Seeing Is Believing: How Hollywood Taught Us to Stop Worrying and Love the Fifties*, focused on the Hollywood films of a single turbulent decade. *Seeing Is Believing* addressed numerous issues that worried Americans during the decade, ranging from sexual relationships to nuclear war and Communist infiltration, through close study of the Hollywood film. The result is a book that illuminates both the filmmakers and the audience—valuable to not just film scholars, but to anyone studying the 1950s in the United States.

By the late 1980s, a larger number of historians were taking part in the conversation between film and history. A special "Forum" section in the December 1988 issue of the *American Historical Review* included contributions by five noted historians. The lead article, "History in Images/ History in Words: Reflections on the Possibility of Really Putting History onto Film," was contributed by film history advocate Robert Rosenstone. In it, he pragmatically addressed the appropriateness of film as a medium for conveying history. He speculated that, perhaps soon, history will be dead to everyone except those who pursue it as a profession. He noted that the audience for the information which professional historians have to deliver or the stories they have to tell is rapidly shrinking: "I fear that as a profession we know less and less how to tell stories that situate us meaningfully in a value-laden world. Stories that matter to people outside our profession. Stories that matter at all."[14] Rosenstone warned that in order to reach any sizeable audience, historians must alter the way in which they function and communicate information. He proposed that movies could, perhaps, play a role in this new strategy:

> Enter film: the great temptation. Film, the contemporary medium still capable of both dealing with the past and holding a large audience. How can we not suspect that this is the medium to use to create narrative histories that will touch large numbers of people? Yet is this dream possible? Can one really put history onto film, history that will satisfy those of us who devote our lives to understanding, analyzing, and recreating the past in words? Or does the use of film necessitate a change in what we mean by history, and would we be willing to make such a change? The issue comes down to this: is it possible to tell historical stories on film and not lose our professional or intellectual souls?[15]

Rosenstone countered the view, held by many of his colleagues, that history consists mainly of "debates between historians."[16] He asserted:

> To present history in a dramatic feature rather than a written text does involve some important trade-offs. . . . Yet the inevitable thinning of data on the screen does not of itself make for poor history. . . . Film lets us see landscapes, hear sounds, witness strong emotions as they are expressed with body and face, or view physical confrontations between individuals or groups.[17]

Addressing historians who clung exclusively to written history, Rosenstone reminded them that "written history is a representation of the past, not the past itself."[18] He conceded that visual history is much different from written history, but argued that it must still be held accountable to standards "consonant with the possibilities of the medium."[19]

Rosenstone urged historians to reconsider film's potential, and to keep in mind that the camera introduces into visual history a variety of components not present in written history. Certain elements of dramatic visual narratives must be "created," but none are, in and of themselves, detrimental to history—"no real violence is done to history by certain additions"[20]—as long as the actual history in question is not derailed, and the "larger" meaning of that history is served. He contended that, if a film tells an accurate story, it can be considered an acceptable historical document, reminding his colleagues that "before Herodotus, there was myth which was a perfectly adequate way of dealing with the past of a tribe, city, or people, adequate in terms of providing a meaningful world in which to live and relate to one's past,"[21] and also suggesting that in contemporary "post-literate" society, visual stories may be the only viable method for relating our past to the general public.

In the same forum, Robert Brent Toplin proposed that many historians have treated "dramatic film as a mirror that reflects the conscious and unconscious values of the producers and their audiences,"[22] an idea he had explored in *Hollywood as Mirror* (1993). Toplin then went on to argue that film does not have to be "complete" to be valuable. It does not need to tell an entire story, thoroughly and accurately, but merely spark viewers' interest and rouse their curiosity about the historical subject, leading to further historical study. As PBS producer Alvin Perlmutter observed: "A film can only introduce a subject. . . . If it is successful, it will bring a subject to the attention of people who did not know much about it before, and it will encourage them to ask questions and seek further information through reading."[23] Quoting Peter Davis, an Academy Award–winning filmmaker, Toplin observed, "Film works well, not in presenting a complete chronology of events, but in exciting feeling and emotions."[24] Thus, film serves the unique role of building upon history, not only to inform but also to entertain the viewing public. He revealed that the famous, montage-inspiring Odessa Steps sequence, which plays such a prominent part in the respected film *Battleship Potemkin*, never happened in real life. Similarly, Richard Attenborough's *Gandhi* (1982) dramatized only selected events and issues in the revered leader's life, but successfully presented Gandhi's spirit, his mission, and the effectiveness of his leadership. It may be suggested that both of these films contribute more to audience's awareness of history than many other more "accurate" texts.

Historian David Herlihy was much less enthusiastic about the potential role of film in history than the other contributors to the forum. He argued that history is "in the main written records, and the traditional function of historical criticism is to collect, evaluate and sort them, in the hope of learning from them what actually happened."[25] In his essay, he maintained that history must remain on the page and suggested that an admonition appear at the beginning of every historical film to warn the audience that what it is about to see is an "interpretation, perhaps not the right interpretation, and usually not the only possible interpretation."[26] For Herlihy, most actual history is unfilmable—motivations are too complex and multidimensional to be captured on the screen. He pointed to the French *Annales* school of historical thought and its disdain for "*histoire événementielle,* the history of happenings"—the history most amenable for filming.[27] Herlihy argued that such an approach presents only the most superficial account of history, but went on to say that "films are superb in representing the visual styles and the textures of the past—values almost impossible to convey in written word. Let the visual serve the visual."[28] Noted historian Hayden White agreed, arguing that no written account of history can be "translated" to film "without significant loss of content," but that reading the visual also requires a different set of skills, and that "modern historians ought to be aware that the analysis of visual images requires a manner of 'reading' quite different from that developed for the study of written documents."[29]

The final contributor to the *American Historical Review* forum was John E. O'Connor. In "History in Images/Images in History: Reflections on the Importance of Film and Television Study for an Understanding of the Past," O'Connor emphasized the film historian's responsibility to the larger community of historical scholars to communicate how film can be relevant to their work.[30] He cited historians' neglect of film by noting that three books had recently been published on the topic of the Dust Bowl of the 1930s but that—despite its integral role in shaping contemporary understanding of the crisis—the landmark short film *The Plow That Broke the Plains* (1936) was allotted only one paragraph in one book, a brief mention in the second, and none at all in the third. O'Connor argued that without consideration of this important film, no book on the Dust Bowl is complete, yet many historians persist in ignoring film's contribution to our understanding of the past.

Film, he noted, also offers multiple viewpoints on historical moments that written history often will not accommodate. To understand racism in Progressive America, one must study not only *Birth of a Nation*, with its portrayals of bestial freed slaves and heroic Ku Klux Klansmen, but also *The Birth of a Race* (1918), which was intended to be the African American answer to Griffith's film. *The Birth of a Race* itself should be examined, O'Connor argued, not in isolation but alongside its makers, its financing, and the wavering commitment of liberal white Americans to its production.[31] He concluded by urging historians to "challenge our students to think analytically about the historical films we show them in the classroom."[32] All history classes should be built around critical thinking, and by making film and television part of that process, "we will have taken a major step toward teaching our students and ourselves to appreciate both history in images and images in history."[33]

The relationship between film and history has, since the early 1990s, become a recognized and legitimate area for historical scholarship, and a steady stream of books and essays on the subject have offered new insights, as well as new cautions. Robert Brent Toplin's *Hollywood as Mirror: Changing Views of "Outsiders" and "Enemies" in American Movies*, for example, considers how themes developed in movies reveal shifts in the public's interests, hopes, fears, and prejudices, and how historical understanding can be advanced by "viewing Hollywood productions in the context of historical change."[34] At the same time, Toplin noted that films are expensive to make, and producers are frequently more concerned with creating popular and profitable films than with accurate depictions of social conditions. Reiterating the point in an essay for *American Historical Review*, he wrote: "Those who communicate through film must find a way to keep viewers in their seats . . . while teachers in the academy have the advantage of a captive audience."[35] He also cautioned that films may "reflect the investments of an elite group, not the general public."[36] Therefore, students of film should exercise caution, lest they "base sweeping conclusions on false assumptions."[37]

Steven Mintz and Randy Roberts' essay collection, *Hollywood's America: United States History through Its Films*, which appeared the same year, echoed the emerging consensus on the relationship between film and history. The book began boldly:

> If you want to know about the United States in the twentieth century, go to the movies. Films represent much more than mass entertainment. Movies even the bad ones—are important sociological and cultural documents. Like any other popular commercial art form, movies both reflect and influence public attitudes. From the very beginning of this century, films have recorded, even shaped American values, beliefs, and even behavior.[38]

The essays that made up the volume ranged from "Coming to Terms with the Vietnam War," in which James S. Olson and Randy Roberts discussed such films as *The Deer Hunter* (1978), *Coming Home* (1979), and *Born on the Fourth of July* (1989), to "Our Movie-Made President," in which Richard Schickel "reviewed" Ronald Reagan's performance as a movie star/politician.

Hollywood's America also included primary source material. The "Postwar Hollywood" section, for example, included excerpts from the House Un-American Activities Committee hearings on communism in Hollywood, and from the court decisions *U.S. v. Paramount* (which barred Hollywood studios from owning theater chains) and *Burstyn v. Wilson* (which declared that movies were a form of speech protected under the First Amendment). Perhaps not coincidentally, the court's ruling in the second case reinforced the editors' views on the significance of film:

> It cannot be doubted that motion pictures are a significant medium for the communication of ideas. They may affect public attitudes and be-

havior in a variety of ways, ranging from direct espousal of a political or social doctrine to the subtle shaping of thought which characterizes all artistic expression. The importance of the motion picture as an organ of public opinion is not lessened by the fact that they are designed to entertain as well as inform.[39]

Over the past two decades, the conversation between historians and film has continued, and while some concerns have remained constant, others have shifted. Most significantly, the question of *how* to use film in the study and teaching of history has gained prominence over the years. This concern is reflected in a broad array of recent work on film and history, such as Alan Marcus's *Celluloid Blackboard: Teaching History with Film* and Alan Metzger's *Teaching History with Film.*

Robert Rosenstone's *Visions of the Past*, an early entry into this discussion, argued that historians deal with film in at least three ways: by studying the history of film as an art and as an industry; by examining films as documents that provide a window into social and cultural concerns of an era; and by investigating an idea "far more radical in its implication: how a visual medium, subject to the conventions of drama and fiction, might be used as a serious vehicle for thinking about our relationship to the past."[40] Film, Rosenstone argues, is an ideal tool for motivating students to become involved in history: "More than the written word, the motion pictures let us stare through a window directly at past events, to experience people and places as if we were there."[41]

In *Past Imperfect: History According to the Movies* (1996), edited by Mark C. Carnes, sixty history-related films are discussed by noted historians and writers. The book is organized chronologically by subject, and so begins with evolutionary biologist Stephen Jay Gould discussing *Jurassic Park* (1992). Later, historian and biographer Antonia Fraser, author of *The Wives of Henry VIII*, considers *Anne of the Thousand Days* (1969)—the story of Henry's second wife, Anne Boleyn—and Dee Brown, author of *Bury My Heart at Wounded Knee*, examines *Fort Apache* (1948) and its depiction of the relationship between the cavalry and the Indians on the Western frontier, calling it "pure John Ford." The book enters the twentieth century with Winston Churchill's premier American biographer, William Manchester, considering *Young Winston* (1972), which chronicles Churchill's dramatic youth. This section contains photos of both of Churchill's parents, Lord Randolph and Lady Churchill, as well as a photo of William Gladstone and a scene of British soldiers in action during a Boer War battle. On the same page, a photograph of the gallant young Churchill in military dress is compared with one of the actor who played him garbed in similar military costume. A chapter on *Hester Street* (1975) deals with historical issues of immigration and assimilation in America by focusing on the lives of Jewish immigrants from Eastern Europe. Included in the chapter's primary materials are a photograph of young Jewish women toiling in a New York sweatshop, and references to Yiddish newspapers and theater. With its many movie and "real-life" illustrations, *Past Imperfect* creates a perfect montage of movies and history.

These attempts to integrate film into the study of history rests, in part, on the idea that films represent the eras in which they are produced—that, for example, Hollywood films produced between 1942 and 1945 offer historians a window on a country at war. The Roosevelt administration's wartime liaison to Hollywood famously asked a single question of any new movie during that time: "Will this film help us win the war?" Even before the United States officially became involved in World War II, however, film reflected—and helped to reinforce Americans' sympathy for Great Britain and determination to come to the aid of the British in their increasingly desperate struggle with Nazi Germany.

Through much of the 1930s, even before Great Britain's entry into the war, Hollywood had stepped up the importation and distribution of British films. Many of the most popular movie stars appearing in American movie theaters were British, including Laurence Olivier, Ronald Colman, Leslie Howard, Greer Garson, and Olivia de Havilland. According to Gore Vidal, "since the movies were by now the principal means of getting swiftly to the masses, Hollywood was not so subtly infiltrated by British propaganda."[42] Vidal contends that, in the 1930s, an entire generation of young Americans had unconsciously sworn allegiance to the English crown in movie theaters.[43] *Foreign Correspondent*, directed by British expatriate Alfred Hitchcock and released in 1940 as Hitler's blitzkrieg overran Western Europe and Britain prepared to make its last stand alone, was little more than a desperate cry for American assistance. When the opportunity to make *Foreign Correspondent* was presented to Hitchcock, he saw it as his way of contributing to Britain's war effort by alerting the United States to the dangers it would soon face:

> Hitchcock wanted to do something for Britain. There is no doubt that
> he felt some guilt for leaving England just as her moment of crisis had
> arrived. . . . He had been expressly asked by the British government to
> continue filmmaking in America. He was also aware of the fact that
> many of the British colony in Hollywood were regarded as desert-
> ers. . . . Somehow he would prove his loyalty to Britain. [44]

Hitchcock employed high drama to convey his point: "He didn't like
message pictures and believed that he could get his ideas about the war
across better by using the thriller format."[45] The film's story line entan-
gled a naive American reporter in European political intrigue, involving
an assassination and a peace conference, which eventually transformed
him into an ardent interventionist. The movie received widespread good
reviews, and earned Hitchcock a telegram of congratulations from presidential advisor Harry Hopkins. Isolationist members of the U.S. Senate
were less pleased, decrying the film as "the kind of pro-Ally propaganda
designed to get America involved in the war"[46] (which, of course, is
precisely what it was). Timing, however, was on the interventionists'
side. By the time Americans saw the film, German bombs were already
falling on England, and star Joel McCrea's impassioned final speech
played like an echo of Edward R. Murrow's tremendously popular radio
reports that began: "This . . . is London."[47]

   After the war, Americans were again in turmoil as they attempted to
adjust to a peace that was uncertain and, at times, perhaps even scarier
than war. Once more, Hollywood was there to record the era's promise
and peril, as Martin Jackson notes in his analysis of William Wyler's *The
Best Years of Our Lives* (1946):

> In its mirroring of the nation's mood in those first years of peace, *The
> Best Years of Our Lives* remains an important piece of evidence re-
> garding the moment in American life when the past had been irretriev-
> ably lost but the future had not yet taken a clear form. . . . For the
> historian, *Best Years* offers an opportunity to grasp the public mood of
> the 1940s. [48]

Wyler's depiction of returning World War II veterans debuted on November 22, 1946, to mixed reviews. Among those who reacted positively
was magazine magnate Henry Luce—publisher of *Time* and *Life*—who

applauded the film's reflection of the realities of newly returned servicemen:

> The veteran, in other words, has actually come home to prosperity and
> happiness, and while it may have taken the skill of the scriptwriters to
> solve [returning veteran Fred] Derry's fictional problems, he was an
> accurate representation of millions of real GIs who also faced the fears
> of unemployment, unwise marriage, and their own futures; they also
> emerge into a better world. For many of those veterans, and their
> families, the late 1940s were in fact "the best years," and they look
> back to those days with deep affection. [49]

The Best Years of Our Lives swept the 1946 Academy Awards, indi-
cating its popular and critical acclaim. Jackson asserts that images such as
Homer—sailor who came home a double amputee—putting his artificial
hands through the garage window in frustration or Fred—a pilot during
the war—walking among rows of surplus warplanes destined for the
scrap yard, are "so bound up in the memories of millions that it is hard to
separate the film from real life."[50] As a result, Jackson notes, "*Best Years*
offers an opportunity to grasp the public mood of the mid-1940s and to
measure the way in which commercial movies both reflect and create the
consciousness of a generation."[51]

In the years between *Foreign Correspondent* and *The Best Years of
Our Lives,* Hollywood released hundreds of films, across every genre,
with a wide range of motivations and styles. How conscientious was
Hollywood, in those films and others set during the war but released long
afterward, in telling the stories of this period in American history? Men
and women who actually lived through the war as immortalized by Hollywood are in an ideal position to comment on Hollywood's credentials as
historian. Those interviewed for this book—veterans of the frontlines and
the home front—were willing to retell their stories and evaluate Hollywood's narratives depicting their war ordeals. Even though the events in
question took place over fifty years ago, they remember the war as if it
were yesterday. Did Hollywood portray World War II the way these vets
experienced it?

2

TOUGH 'OMBRES AND *BATTLEGROUND*

Hollywood produced over three hundred movies about World War II while it was taking place, and has produced hundreds more since. [1] Long after their original releases, these films continue to reach new generations of viewers—including many too young to have known the war—on television, home video, and the Internet. Every Memorial Day weekend, the Second World War is fought around the clock on cable networks such as AMC and Turner Classic Movies. The popularity of these films, and their role in shaping viewers' understanding of World War II, raises questions about the relationship between Hollywood warfare and the real war. Was the war really as it was depicted in the movies? Did the war movies shown during the first years of World War II affect the young men who enlisted later? Have any postwar movies accurately portrayed the war? As a World War II combat veteran, Harry Miller of Bloomington, Illinois, is in a unique position to offer some answers. [2]

Miller was fifteen years old when Pearl Harbor was bombed, and he was drafted when he turned eighteen in 1944. Asked if the war movies he saw during his high school years had any effect on him, he was very blunt: "Yeah, movies like *Wake Island* (1942) and *Guadalcanal Diary* (1943) made me hate the Japanese." Hollywood portrayals of the Japanese as crazed fanatics and Nazis as sneering, murderous thugs did not, however, make him "gung ho" about fighting the enemy. He considered Charlie Chaplin's satire *The Great Dictator* (1940) hilarious, but beyond that, Hollywood war movies of the early 1940s had no distinct effect on him. The newsreels that accompanied the war movies—which included footage shot on actual battlefields—were another matter. The "real" war looked exceedingly uninviting to Miller, and like his buddies, he was not anxious to get involved. His local draft board had different plans, however, and he was inducted into the Army soon after he turned eighteen.

After he returned home, a combat veteran, Miller preferred not to watch war movies; he had seen the real thing. The 1949 drama *Battleground*, however, makes a bold claim of being an authentic, realistic, and lifelike depiction of an event—the Battle of the Bulge—that Miller experienced firsthand. Miller agreed to watch the film and discuss how it compared with his own wartime experiences.

The Battle of the Bulge was Nazi Germany's last great offensive of the war. It began on December 16, 1944, when thirteen German divisions—200,000 men backed by over 600 armored vehicles and 1,600 artillery pieces—smashed into a thinly defended section of the Allied lines in the heavily wooded Ardennes region of Belgium. Taken completely by surprise, and deprived of air support by winter weather that kept Allied aircraft grounded, 63,000 American troops fought a desperate holding action amid deep snow and bitter cold. At the edges of the German advance—Elsenborn Ridge in the north, and the village of Bastogne in the south—they were able to hold their positions. In the center, they were forced steadily backward, creating an inward bulge in the American lines that gave the battle its name.

Two days before Christmas, 1944, the tide of the battle began to turn. Unfavorable terrain and tenacious resistance had delayed the German forces' advance, enabling the Allies to rush reinforcements to the area. On December 23, the weather improved enough for American aircraft to take to the skies, attacking German troops and delivering supplies to hard-pressed defenders. The bulge reached its greatest extent on Christmas Day, then gradually began to collapse on itself. Troops under the command of General George Patton broke through the German forces surrounding Bastogne on the afternoon of December 26, relieving the 101st Airborne Division. Thrust and counterthrust continued for another month, but the momentum of the German advance was spent. What remained of the German forces gradually fell back to the heavily fortified Siegfried Line on the French-German border, where they prepared to fight on the defensive for the remainder of the war.

Hitler had envisioned the Ardennes campaign as a second blitzkrieg, a bold thrust that would split the Allied lines and put the Belgian port of

Antwerp in German hands. The target was carefully chosen: the Anglo-American forces that threatened Germany from the west were supplied, primarily, through Antwerp. Had it fallen, the end of the war would have been significantly delayed, with potentially catastrophic results for the Allies. The attack failed, but the cost of turning it back was high. Over 19,000 American troops were killed, 47,500 wounded, and 23,000 captured or missing, making the Battle of the Bulge the bloodiest engagement fought by the U.S. Army during the war.

Produced by Dore Schary for MGM, *Battleground* was directed by World War I veteran William Wellman, who had earlier won recognition for directing the war films *Wings* (1927) and *The Story of GI Joe* (1945).[3] The screenwriter, Bob Pirosh, had been a soldier in the Battle of the Bulge and "had come out of the war with notes on his experience and a desire to do a movie about the Battle of the Bulge."[4] In April 1947, Pirosh returned to the battlefields where he had fought. He decided to portray the activities of one squad of riflemen—"without heroics, without fancy speeches, without a phony romance." He wanted to write a picture that would "ring true to the men [who had fought there] and which would not be an insult to the memory of those we left there." Pirosh felt that the story of one squad was, in a sense, "the story of all squads. . . . The important thing is what did it do to us? How did we feel?"[5]

The filmmakers who shaped *Battleground*, particularly Schary, were determined to make their war movie as realistic as possible. To this end, Wellman decided, "I'll make a film about a very tired group of guys."[6] General Anthony McAuliffe (who had commanded the 101st Airborne at Bastogne, and gained immortality when he replied "Nuts!" to a German suggestion to surrender) recommended a former subordinate, Lieutenant Colonel Harry W. O. Kinnard, as technical advisor for the film.[7] In *The War Film*, Norman Kagan says of *Battleground* that

> The accent was on plausibility: the snow-covered battleground, the clumsy, heavy-coated dogfaces slogging along or digging foxholes or in a swift, confused fire fight with English-speaking Nazi infiltrators. . . . *Battleground* is really most about the look of combat, what Ernie Pyle called "a look that is the display room for what lies beyond it; exhaustion, lack of sleep, tension for too long, weariness that is too great, fear beyond fear, misery to the point of numbness."[8]

This movie has no big explosions, airplanes, tanks, strife among the men and officers, or any of a dozen other elements that routinely appear in a successful war movie. Instead, *Battleground* is a slice of the real war seen through the eyes of a few common soldiers on the frontline. It tells the story of the 327th Glider Infantry Regiment, 101st Airborne Division, as they battle German forces in the Ardennes. The courage and camaraderie of the men is tested time and again as they endure attack and counterattack, only to be surrounded by the enemy, making what *Stars and Stripes* called "a heroic stand." Under siege and down to their last rounds of ammunition, the 101st is rescued by Allied fighters, but only after sustaining devastating losses. Still, as they are being relieved, the bedraggled, war-torn company stands tall on their march out of battle, proud to have served.

In *War Movies*, Jay Hyams praised *Battleground* as the best of the postwar period, in spite of the fact that "there are no contrived heroics, and the fear and confusion of the soldiers are made clear. . . . They know

Figure 2.1. Members of the 327th Glider Regiment, 101st Airborne Division, face the Siege of Bastogne during the Battle of the Bulge.

only what is happening in their small sector. The war is reduced to a series of bitter contests for short stretches of snowy ground."[9]

The movie did well at the box office in 1949 and won two Academy Awards—one for script and one for photography. Today the only well-known actors in the film are Van Johnson and James Whitmore, who convincingly portray regular combat soldiers. Ricardo Montalban plays the Hispanic American soldier who provided the required Hollywood ethnic diversity.

Most Americans born after 1945 have picked up their war history primarily from such "classic" wartime films as *A Yank in the RAF* (1941), *Mrs. Miniver* (1942), or *Sahara* (1943), or from more recent—but equally "Hollywoodized"—pictures like *The Longest Day* (1962) and *Patton* (1970). Does *Battleground* live up to its promise to show what World War II was really like? Harry Miller—who, as a teenage infantryman assigned to the 90th Division, found himself exchanging fire with Germans in the Ardennes in January 1945—was an ideal person to provide answers to this question.

Basic training completed, Miller arrived at his home in Bloomington, Illinois, on Christmas morning 1944, looking forward to a two-week furlough before shipping out to Europe. Later that day, however, he received an official telegram: the rapidly changing situation in the Ardennes meant that every available soldier was needed, and all leave was canceled. Private Miller reported to Camp Kilmer, New Jersey, where he "drew his weapon" and other combat equipment. Soon afterward, he was boarding the troop-laden *Queen Elizabeth* at her berth in lower Manhattan, as a band played on the dock. The former luxury liner was barely recognizable: her prewar finery had been stripped away, replaced with dull gray paint and four-tiered bunks and mess halls to accommodate the troops. She retained the massive engines that had made her the fastest ship on the prewar North Atlantic, however, and the voyage to Scotland took only four days. The journey into battle was very quiet, Miller recalls: "We all had our own thoughts." They traveled by train to England, crossed the English Channel, and were loaded onto boxcars near the French port of Le Havre. Like the soldiers in *Battleground*, they were brought by trucks to a point near the frontlines where a "couple of guys came and got me and took me up."

Miller noted that *Battleground*'s set, which was supposed to be the frontline in Belgium, looked perfectly authentic—"the same snow." When asked what combat was really like, he responded:

> Someone described it right once when he said "War is hell!" Especially when you are young like I was, only eighteen years old and on the front line, you are scared to death, and that is all there is to it. Thank God for the older guys who took the younger guys under their wings until you got a little combat-hardened. After you are out there for a couple of months, you are a veteran; you are hardened.

Battleground depicts the same process, with Jim Layton—like Miller, a young man fresh from basic training—learning how to handle himself in combat by using the veteran Holley (Van Johnson) as a role model. Asked about the camaraderie that the squad in *Battleground* shared, and the way the men seemed to care for each other, the former soldier concurred. When he first went on the line, his sergeant "looked after" him and made sure that the "kid" stayed close by. Later, a newcomer from Harrisburg, Pennsylvania, came up to the line, and Miller watched out for him until he became acclimated.

This process of informal education had to happen quickly, since new replacements were walking into the midst of an ongoing campaign, and fighting could break out at any moment. Miller's first experience of combat came on his third or fourth day on the line. "You were pretty busy, with no time to think," he recalled. Knowing what to do, and having buddies for support, was essential to survival. Even with those advantages, however, nothing was guaranteed. Miller recalled:

> A couple [of battles] come to mind where I lost good friends. We were in the woods and were being bombarded, and, of course, one of the worst places to be is in the woods where bombs explode the trees. I think all of us were pretty frightened that day. There were a lot of guys who just broke down; their nerves were just shattered, they were weeping uncontrollably. A couple became shell-shocked and they went in the wrong direction and headed towards the enemy instead of trying to get away like most of us were; we were trying to get the heck out of those woods.

Battleground, unlike most Hollywood war movies, treats this kind of psychological breakdown as a fact of life on the frontlines. In the film, during a heavy shelling ("incoming mail"), a frantic soldier jumps out of his foxhole and runs in the wrong direction. Watching him, another soldier comments: "Some people just can't take it."

World War II movies are famous for depicting even military units as cross-sections of America. In Hollywood's version of the war, every bomber crew and infantry platoon seems to include a "college boy" and a factory worker, a New Yorker, a Southerner, and a person of color. *Battleground*, though it rejects many war-movie conventions, acknowledges this one in its inclusion of Private Roderigues, a Latino from Los Angeles. In regard to his own platoon, Miller said, Hollywood got it right. When it was formed during World War I, the 90th Infantry had consisted mostly of men from Texas and Oklahoma, but in World War II its members came from throughout the United States.[10] The division's red-on-khaki insignia, a superimposed T and O, once stood for Texas-Oklahoma, but by 1944 it represented the division's nickname: the "Tough 'Ombres." The Army was the first contact Miller, born and raised in central Illinois, had with men from different ethnic groups and different parts of the country. His comrades-in-arms included Jews, Latinos, a Native American, and a young Puerto Rican named Perez, who was killed in action. "They were all your comrades," Miller recalled. "They were your buddies. They tried to help you stay alive, and you tried to help them stay alive. It's hard to explain the feeling you have for the men you are in combat with. It's like nothing else. It's hard to explain." One of *Battleground*'s strengths, he noted, is its portrayal of the unique bond that develops between men who experience combat together.

Mail from home helped to maintain the different, but equally important, bond between soldiers and those they left behind. *Battleground*'s "mail call" scenes, in which the soldiers receive letters from home even though they are on the embattled frontlines, might seem like Hollywood dramatics, but for Miller they rang true. Mail, he said, was delivered to his unit daily, no matter where it was. The mail carrier went from foxhole to foxhole if necessary, and every soldier got his letters from home, even though he might not have the time or the light required to read them. Just as in the movies, however, news on the war's progress came late (if at all) to the soldiers on the frontline. The soldiers in *Battleground* discover that they are engaged in the "heroic defense of Bastogne" only when they read about it in a days-old Army newspaper. The men in Miller's real-life unit were similarly out of touch, but they did hear lots of rumors, especially

rumors about General George Patton, the commander of the U.S. Third
Army to which the 90th Infantry belonged. One such rumor was that
Patton—famous for his insistence on spit-and-polish even in combat
zones—wanted his soldiers to be clean-shaven and neatly dressed for
burial, just in case.

When watching *Battleground*, Miller immediately noticed the soldiers
with their feet wrapped in bandages and rags because—like Washington's
soldiers at Valley Forge—their boots had worn out. The sight was a
familiar one to him, and he said that most of the soldiers evacuated from
the front for reasons other than wounds were suffering from frostbite.
Every fresh replacement who went up to the frontline carried an entire
new set of clothes to be given to the men who were on the line already.
The frontline soldiers were "ecstatic" with the new clothes, particularly
the latest style of combat boots, but—as in the movie, GI gas masks were
immediately discarded—they were, as Miller succinctly put it, "a pain."

The Battle of the Bulge veteran also gave the film credit for its depictions of soldiers sleeping out in the snow: no tents, no shelter, just foxholes. Miller himself slept outside every night, except for one night when
his outfit was able to sleep in a bombed-out church, a real luxury after
months of nights in a hole. No matter how (relatively) comfortable their
surroundings, however, no one at the front ever really slept well. Soldiers
were always tense, waiting for the unexpected. Every man took his turn
standing guard sometime between dusk and dawn, so guard duty usually
interrupted any hope of restful sleep. Miller did remember getting some
good, uninterrupted sleep once, though:

> We heard that the war had ended. Most of us just climbed off our
> vehicles and went to the ditch and laid down and went to sleep. We
> were all pretty tired. That was one of the big reliefs when the war was
> over—that you could close your eyes without fear.

Until the war ended, however, exhaustion was part of the frontline soldier's everyday life. *Battleground*'s authenticity comes, in part, from its
ability to capture the bone-weariness of the soldiers.

Between the time Miller arrived in Belgium and the time he could
finally close his eyes without fear, he participated in three major battles
and innumerable skirmishes. These skirmishes usually took place when
U.S. patrol reconnoitering the enemy's positions ran into a German patrol
doing the same. Patrols from the opposing armies tried to avoid each

other, but occasionally they did not succeed and fire was exchanged, sometimes lethally.

When the Germans had "broken through" Allied lines in late 1944, they had captured U.S. Army uniforms as well as jeeps, trucks, and other American vehicles. English-speaking Germans dressed in GI uniforms and driving GI jeeps attempted to infiltrate the American lines. A soldier couldn't be sure "who was GI and who was German." Passwords, Miller noted, were the only thing separating friend from foe. As a result, they were carefully chosen to distinguish native English speakers from those whose first language was German, often containing the letter "w," which German speakers pronounced as "v." Returning the correct password— the only sure way for Americans to identify themselves to each other— was a matter of life and death. One relatively humorous scene from *Battleground* makes this point by showing an officer trying to convince members of a U.S. patrol that he is an American, and not a German imposter. The patrol members are suspicious, and—using another standard method of identifying "real" Americans—quiz him about baseball. No sports fan, the officer is on the verge of being shot as a Nazi spy when he is able to answer an intricate question about musical comedy and pinup star Betty Grable, thus confirming that he is indeed a red-blooded American man.

Battleground ends with the relief of Bastogne by Patton's tanks, and the withdrawal of the platoon's surviving members for much-needed rest behind the lines. Miller's war, however, continued after the Battle of the Bulge ended. He took part in the battles for the Rhine and central Germany, earning the Silver Star for "gallantry in combat" when he captured a group of "forward observers" whose job was to direct the fire of German artillery. Even in the last stages of the war, he recalled, the fighting was ferocious. His unit fought house-to-house during the crossing of the Rhine, and in the city of Mainz, U.S. soldiers found German women operating the artillery and children as young as thirteen bearing arms— attempting to defend the Fatherland and willing to "fight to the death for Hitler." When asked how Allied soldiers responded to children with guns, Miller simply replied that kids, too, could be dangerous. The most tenacious of all were members of the elite SS—the military wing of the Nazi Party—whom Miller helped to capture on three different occasions. He remembers them as very Aryan-looking officers, always highly decorated, and remembers hating them because they were the most arrogant people he had ever seen. "Boy, they didn't want to be captured," Miller said, recalling that they spit in the faces of their American captors. Eventually, one SS man spit in the wrong American face and died for his act of defiance.

After Germany's surrender, Miller—since promoted to corporal—remained in Germany as part of the U.S. military government, acting as chief clerk in both Landshut and Vilshoffen. His assignment in occupied Germany was evocative of the 1948 film *A Foreign Affair,* but when questioned about his own postwar affairs in Germany, Miller stated that he never ran into anyone like the film's stars, Marlene Dietrich or Jean Arthur. As a matter of fact, for the first six months after the war's end, American soldiers were forbidden—under threat of arrest and imprisonment—from fraternizing with Germans. Consequently, Miller spent most of his nights playing cards with his buddies and "talking about going home." As a soldier in *Battleground* suggests, the real meaning of PFC is not "private first class" but "praying for civilian."

Summing up his thoughts on *Battleground,* Miller agreed with those who have called it a realistic war film. From the buddy system to the mail delivery, the frostbite, and the fear of Germans impersonating GIs, it mirrored his own experiences on the frontlines in the Ardennes. Miller even recalled that he had worn a knife in his pant leg, just as Van Johnson did in the film, though—unlike the actor/soldier—he used his not in combat, but only for "peeling potatoes and trying to look tough." The terror of being under artillery bombardment also resonated, as did the grim observation made by one of the soldiers in *Battleground*: "It was the shell you didn't hear that got you." Ultimately for Miller, the most realistic detail of all was the sound of the howitzer shells: "You never forget that sound. That sound brought it all back."

Since the end of the war, Harry Miller prefers not to talk about his distinguished war record. When pressed about his medals and ribbons (displayed in an out-of-the-way room in his basement) he offered no details about the action that earned him the Silver Star. The ribbon that he was most proud of was the Combat Infantry Badge: the blue-and-silver sign of a soldier who had met the enemy in combat and survived. "That's the one all the guys wanted." The next insignia that he pointed out was the "T-O" shoulder patch that marked him as a Tough 'Ombre—the same patch that had been worn by him and all his comrades-in-arms, both the living and the dead. He prefers not to dwell on that time in his life when his country sent him to a foreign continent to fight a war, even though the war played a significant part in his life and will always be with him. When he gets together with other combat veterans, they prefer to remember the funny things that happened to them. Combat was something that he just had to do, like it or not.

The quiet soldiers, Miller explained, were the ones who did the real fighting. "They just did their jobs." The ones who talked big and swaggered—imitating the kind of larger-than-life movie heroes played by John Wayne—were unpopular and definitely not heroes. There was, in Miller's view, no glory in the war; it was simply "you fight or die." His platoon, he said, was just a bunch of guys scared to death, cold, tired, and all with only one wish: to go home. *Battleground*, in his opinion, communicates this essential aspect of war. It is a film about the quiet soldiers—frightened, freezing, exhausted, homesick men doing a job as well as they could, in spite of their horrible circumstances.

Asked if it had been hard for him to readjust to home and civilian life, Miller smiled and said that, after returning to Illinois, he wanted to finish his senior year of high school. He needed only four additional credits in order to graduate. For his eighteen months in Europe, his three battle stars, and his role in defeating Nazi Germany, the school system awarded him two of those four required credits. War may be hell, but it doesn't excuse you from chemistry class.

3

CARRIERS AND KAMIKAZES:
WING AND A PRAYER

Jim Hoisington graduated from Wheaton College in the summer of 1941. Because Wheaton was a conservative religious school (Billy Graham was in the class behind him), Hoisington had not been able to see any of the movies that anticipated America's entry into the war raging in Europe and Asia. In September 1941, Hoisington signed up for the U.S. Naval Reserve. Thanks to a government-sponsored program in which he had participated while still in college, he was already a licensed pilot. Hoisington knew he wanted to fly if the United States entered the war: "I didn't want to walk."[1] Even today, he's not really sure why he chose the Navy over the Army Air Corps—maybe it was because his father had been in the Navy. Also, he quips that his height was a cause for concern: he is a tall man, and thought that the cockpit of the Army fighters might not give him enough leg room. In any case, the World War II veteran has never regretted his choice. Hoisington recalled his Navy days spent on three different aircraft carriers and compared his true-life experiences with Hollywood's version of life on a carrier as shown in *Wing and a Prayer* (1944).

Hoisington was called up to active duty less than a week after the Japanese attack on Pearl Harbor and attended basic training at the Glenview Naval Air Station near Chicago. He chose dive bombers over fighters—which he saw as more dangerous—out of consideration for his parents and his fiancée, Lois. He continued his flight training in Corpus Christie, Texas, where he received his Navy wings. According to Hoisington, "At 10 a.m. that Friday morning [September 18, 1942] we got our officers' commission and our wings. At 2 that afternoon (and Lois doesn't like to hear this) I got my wings clipped when we got married." After a year of additional training, Hoisington found himself in the South Pacific, stationed aboard the aircraft carrier *Enterprise*. Later he was transferred to other carriers, the *Intrepid* and then the *Hancock*.

Carriers, along with submarines, were the principal offensive weapons of the war in the Pacific. Prewar naval strategy had been built around massed fleets of battleships mounting 14-inch or 16-inch cannon and protected by thick layers of hardened steel armor, but Pearl Harbor overturned those calculations in a matter of hours. The Japanese attack put the battleships of the U.S. Pacific fleet out of action, some for weeks or months, others for years, and a few—like the ill-fated *Arizona*—forever. Deprived of what it believed were its most powerful assets, the Navy turned to its aircraft carriers, which by chance and military necessity had been away from Pearl Harbor on December 7, to fill the gap. To the surprise of everyone but aviation-minded officers like Admiral William Halsey, they proved more than equal to the task. The first air strike against the Japanese mainland—sixteen twin-engine Army bombers commanded by Colonel Jimmy Doolittle—was launched from the *Hornet* in April 1942, and planes from *Lexington* and *Yorktown* thwarted a planned invasion of Australia at the Battle of the Coral Sea the following month. The turning point of the Pacific War—the Battle of Midway on June 1–3, 1942—was also decided by air power: American carrier pilots sank four Japanese carriers (two-thirds of the striking force that had attacked Pearl Harbor) and ended expansion in the Pacific for good.

The American naval offensive that began in the summer of 1942 and ended three years later at a surrender ceremony in Tokyo Bay was dominated by carriers. Five of the Navy's eight prewar carriers had been sunk by the end of 1942 (*Enterprise*, Hoisington's first posting, was one of the survivors), but a steady stream of new ones like *Intrepid* and *Hancock*—bigger, faster, and more capable—made up the losses many times over. New carrier-based aircraft also entered the war in late 1942 and 1943: Hellcat fighters, Avenger torpedo bombers, and Helldiver diver bombers replaced the now-outdated machines that had triumphed at Coral Sea and Midway. Carrier task forces built around these state-of-the-art weapons swept across the central and southwest Pacific in 1943 and 1944. Initially, they focused on sinking Japanese warships, attacking and then slipping away into the Pacific before land-based Japanese aircraft could reach them. Over time, however, the Navy's use of carriers grew bolder and more confident. Under the command of veteran carrier commander (and pioneer naval aviator) Admiral Marc Mitscher, the ships of the Fast Carrier Task Force attacked Japanese shore installations—including heavily fortified ones like Truk—blowing up buildings and runways, and sweeping land-based aircraft from the skies, along with most of Japan's dwindling pool of veteran pilots. In the fall of 1944, American carriers broke the back of the Japanese fleet at the Battle of Leyte Gulf, and sent the battleships *Yamato* and *Musashi*—the largest ever built—to the bottom of the Pacific, clearing the way for the recapture of the Philippines and the assaults on Iwo Jima and Okinawa in early 1945.

Wing and a Prayer represents Hollywood's wartime depiction of the day-to-day life of Navy carrier pilots. Directed by Henry Hathaway and released in 1944, at the height of the global conflict, it mixes Hollywood-style drama with actual combat footage and documentary-like footage shot aboard the *Yorktown*, an *Essex*-class carrier, during its shakedown cruise. Its portrayal of life aboard a floating airfield—a composite of

Figure 3.1. **Watching the skies from aboard *Carrier X* in *Wing and a Prayer*.**

adventures from such ships as the *Enterprise, Lexington,* and *Hornet*—closely parallels Hoisington's own experiences. *Wing and a Prayer* was nominated for an Academy Award for Best Screenplay in 1944, and has received much critical acclaim: Leonard Maltin awarded it three stars, describing it as a "fine WW2 actioner of life aboard a navy aircraft carrier,"[2] and a September 1944 *Newsweek* review praised it as

> a dramatic detailed almost documentary record of hard work and heroism aboard an aircraft carrier in the early days of the Pacific war. . . . The director, Henry Hathaway, and a camera crew spent seven weeks aboard a carrier shooting 50,000 feet of factual footage. The Navy came through with official shots and soundtracks . . . Hathaway has used both to good advantage along with authentic battle sets and a reasonable facsimile of the emotions of 3,000 odd men involved.[3]

Similarly, the September 1944 issue of *Commonweal* magazine commended the realism of the film's scenes: "Through some extraordinary photography . . . we are made to feel that we are participating on the ship and in the air above it."[4]

The film describes itself as a salute to the Navy men who helped to cripple the Japanese fleet in the Battle of Midway.[5] It is set in the six months immediately following the attack on Pearl Harbor, when American carriers were coming into their own as a striking force in the Pacific, and references the actual battles of the Coral Sea and Midway. Its central plot involves an elaborate ruse in which *Carrier X* plays a central role. The ship is assigned, by an unnamed admiral, to zigzag across the central Pacific, making contact with the Japanese at widely separated locations, but not engaging with them. The purpose of the plan is to convince the Japanese that they are encountering a number of different carriers, and that the Pacific Fleet is widely scattered. The Japanese fall for the trap, and send their own carriers to attack Midway, which they assume will be undefended. Instead, they find the American carriers waiting—massed, ready, and joined at last by *Carrier X*—and are soundly defeated.

While discussing *Wing and a Prayer*, Hoisington found much to commend, but also noted a number of flaws, both major and minor. He immediately disputed the fictitious mission assigned to *Carrier X*, noting that after the Battle of the Coral Sea, the Navy had only three carriers available in the Pacific and the Navy would never have endangered one in this manner. The Navy *was* weak and scattered in the spring of 1942, and there was no need to convince the Japanese of the fact because they already knew it. The attack on Midway—planned by Admiral Isoroku Yamamoto, who had also orchestrated the Pearl Harbor operation—was designed to take advantage of that weakness, striking at the vital base before the Pacific Fleet could make good its losses.

The U.S. Navy's real advantage at Midway was that its cryptographers had broken the Japanese naval code, and could read the communications that passed between senior commanders and the fleet. They not only knew that Japan intended to attack Midway, but also when and how the attack was scheduled to take place, and could plan their defenses accordingly. All of this was, however, top secret in 1944—something the filmmakers could not have known and the Navy would never have publicly admitted. The story of *Carrier X*, a decoy that fooled the Japanese into thinking the U.S. Navy was weak, was a convenient fiction to explain what "really" happened at Midway.

Hoisington also noted that the planes shown in the movie, which is set in early 1942, were the later, more powerful models that came into use later in the war and were being flown from American carriers at the time the film was set. In addition, he pointed out that "in one quick shot of what was supposed to be a Zero [Japanese fighter], they used an SNJ, a U.S. Navy trainer."[6] Given that the movie was produced in wartime, however, Hoisington regarded these errors as understandable and excusable. While the country was at war, substitutes for a great many things had to be found, and Hollywood was not exempt from this wartime inconvenience. Ironically, the substitution of readily available aircraft for scarce, but historically accurate, ones continued long after the war. Most of the Japanese aircraft that survived the war were scrapped under the terms of the peace treaty, leaving a handful in museums but virtually none flyable. Trainers like the SNJ and its Army equivalent (the AT-6) survived in large numbers, however, and so continued to "play" Zeroes in movies such as *Tora! Tora! Tora!* (1970) and *Midway* (1976), until computer graphics (like those used in the 2001 film *Pearl Harbor*) made such impersonations unnecessary.

For the most part, Hoisington considered the scenes shot on the carrier to be authentic-looking, but noted that the movie's carrier was much cleaner and less cluttered than the real ones he served on. He illustrated the point by producing a picture of the ready room—a briefing room where pilots gathered before missions, and were briefed on weather, courses, targets, and other vital details—on the *Hancock*. It was jam-packed with the pilots' gear: flying helmets, charts, parachutes, and the yellow life vests that pilots nicknamed "Mae Wests" because—when in-flated—they gave the wearer a silhouette reminiscent of the buxom co-medienne. Also, he observed,

> Smoking was much more common than shown in this movie. The ready room that we used on the old *Enterprise* in late 1943 did not have the ventilation evident in this movie. The smoke was so thick that my eyes would run with tears so that I could hardly see the blackboard at the front of the room to copy the directions for the flight. [7]

In the film, two pilots share what appears to be a very comfortable room on *Carrier X*, accommodations that were familiar to Hoisington. "The living quarters looked correct for officers above the rank of ensign," he said, and went on to note that, compared with the conditions most other soldiers and sailors were forced to endure, his were quite pleasant: "On board ship we had clean quarters and usually good food. It was kind of like living in a hotel on the big carriers." [8]

Life aboard both aircraft carriers—both fictional and factual—in-volved recreational activities impossible on smaller ships or in frontline foxholes. In the film, Dana Andrews's character invites a forlorn, grounded pilot to play "acey-deucy," and the pilot eagerly responds to the invitation. Hoisington explained that acey-deucy was not a poker or dice game, but rather a variation of backgammon that was extremely popular in the Navy, especially aboard ships. The movie characters are also de-picted enjoying a film—the musical comedy *Tin Pan Alley* (1940), star-ring Betty Grable and (not coincidentally) produced by the same studio as *Wing and a Prayer*. Hoisington mentioned watching many movies while stationed on aircraft carriers—their cavernous "hangar decks," where planes were stored and repaired, worked well as makeshift theaters—and remembered one movie being interrupted for a military emergency. Doz-ens of soldiers and sailors in Hollywood war films, and tens of thousands in real life, brought Betty Grable into their quarters by way of her famous pinup photo. Showing the famously long-legged star in a white swimsuit and high heels, it was the most popular photo of the war, eclipsing a shot of Rita Hayworth kneeling on a rumpled bed in a slinky nightgown. Hoisington, newly married, had neither Grable nor Hayworth on the wall of his cabin, preferring a photo of his wife, and he did not notice what his fellow pilots hung on the walls of their rooms.

Hoisington observed that, although the equipment of the movie's actor-pilots, along with their "authentic Navy luggage and their clothes looked correct,"[9] they wore their gear in ways that—to a real naval aviator—looked subtly unrealistic. The actors, for example, almost always had their flight goggles pushed up onto their heads—no doubt all the better to see those beautiful Hollywood faces—instead of keeping them over their eyes the way real pilots did. Hoisington also noted, "They seemed to wear their Mae Wests and their parachute harnesses most of the time in the movie, even when they weren't necessary."[10] When viewing the segment of the film where the pilots prepared for bed, he said that "changing into . . . pajamas [as the characters in the movie did] was not very common. Most of us slept in our T-shirts and shorts."[11]

When Hoisington was asked about the realism of the actors' performances, he responded that "they're pretty good." Commenting on Bingo Harper, the ultra-aloof and uncompromising flight commander played by Don Ameche, Hoisington acknowledged that most commanders preferred to keep a bit of emotional distance between themselves and their men. Nevertheless, he recalled one commander who regularly shared drunken exploits with his men when they were on leave. The grounding of one pilot for psychological, as well as physical, reasons also rang true. Hoisington said that he was aware of men who requested to be permanently grounded and assigned to less stressful jobs, and recalled an episode involving a shipmate: "One of my friends in the dive bomber squadron had to make a water landing at night and it was a pretty rough experience for him. He was released to return to the States . . . and decided he had enough flying."[12] When questioned about the authenticity of pilot "Beezy Bessemer" (Richard Jaeckel) having lied about his age to enlist in the Navy, Hoisington replied that he didn't run into any underage men in his squadron, but did know a man who had lied about his marital status in order to qualify for flight training. He explained that before the war started, the Navy Air Corps only admitted single men, but after Pearl Harbor that rule was scrapped.

The movie's portrayal of a pilot ignoring a wave-off—landing even after he had been ordered to go around and make another approach—was, for Hoisington, its most unrealistic piece of characterization. He declared that such an incident would never have happened, explaining that he and the other Navy pilots he knew were trained to unquestioningly follow the instructions of the LSO—the landing signal officer, who stood on the edge of the deck and guided the pilots to a safe landing—and it never would have occurred to them to ignore him. The LSO's instructions were equivalent to orders, and a real pilot who disregarded a wave-off would have been grounded—for life.

The squadron in *Wing and a Prayer* includes a former movie star, Hallam "Oscar" Scott (William Eythe); however, he is just one of the guys in the squadron, and his buddies enjoy teasing him about knowing Betty Grable. The situation in Hoisington's squadron was reversed: he remembered a gunner in his squadron who was quite a "card," named Richard Boone, who, more than a decade after the war, went on to star in the hit Western television series, *Have Gun, Will Travel*. The squadron did have a celebrity close to hand, but not one from Hollywood: "we had a well-known Navy man who was commander of our Air Group," Hoisington remembered. "His name was Butch O'Hare and we have an airport near Chicago named after him."[13] O'Hare was, in fact, more than simply "well-known" in 1943: he was the Navy's first ace, first Medal of Honor winner, and first national hero of the war. He had come to national attention a year earlier when, flying from the *Lexington*, he had single-handedly taken on a squadron of six attacking twin-engined bombers, shooting down or driving off every one.

During the time he was stationed on the *Enterprise*, the *Intrepid*, and the *Hancock*, Hoisington flew innumerable missions, some that were fairly routine surveillance or patrolling flights, and others that were anything but routine. On March 31, 1945, Hoisington was involved in a strike on an airfield called Yontan, on Okinawa. The next day, during a review of the strike, "the Air Group Commander, Henry Miller, commented that we [Hoisington and his gunner] had found more targets than anyone else on Okinawa, or something to that effect. It made my day to have recognition and encouragement like that from the Air Group Commander."[14] The film's improbable main plot, however, involves *Carrier X* being under strict order to make contact with the enemy—see and be seen—but not engage with them. The men in the film follow these orders, but are unaware that they are part of an elaborate deception, and so grow increasingly frustrated with the lack of action. Only at the end of the film do all the pilots take off for Midway and the real war, pleased to be involved in the action at last.

Flying from a pitching, moving steel "airfield" in the middle of the ocean was dangerous, and mishaps were common. As happens in the film, Hoisington said, they most often occurred during takeoff and landing. One of the running subplots in the film involves egotistical pilots who think they don't need to follow orders, but soon find out that on *Carrier X* mavericks are not tolerated. Ensign Brainard (Harry Morgan) is grounded for dropping a practice bomb too close to the ship, and "Oscar" Scott, who is consistently casual about adhering to standard procedures, runs out of fuel after the final battle and is forced to ditch in the sea. One of the crashes in *Wing and a Prayer* was caused by a pilot Hoisington labeled a "hot shot"—a pilot who thought he was a lot more skillful than he actually was; Ensign Cunningham (Kevin O'Shea) disregards proper takeoff procedures and, as a result, crashes into the sea. Hoisington recalled a similar landing accident:

> I got out and made it to the edge of the flight deck when one of the hot shot pilots of VF-6 [the *Enterprise*'s fighter squadron] made a bad landing and bounced over the barriers and landed on the planes behind mine. A number of planes were thrown over the side as junk. Our squadron pilots were quite put out because several of our Corsairs were wrecked and discarded. [15]

The movie pilots frequently have to put their planes down in the ocean. Hoisington recalled a similar experience when enemy fire damaged his plane and forced him into a water landing: "I estimate we had twenty seconds before the plane sank from beneath us. We both had life jackets called 'Mae Wests' so we inflated them. . . . The water was warm because we were near the equator, like a nice bath temperature." [16] Fortunately, this incident took place off the coast of an island where American troops were landing, and an empty landing craft eventually picked up Hoisington and his gunner.

As the Japanese grew more desperate in their losing battle, suicide attacks became more and more frequent. Isolated incidents of pilots crashing their severely damaged planes into enemy ships—sacrificing their lives in the hope of inflicting mortal damage on an enemy vessel—had occurred on both sides during the first years of the war, but in 1945 Japan turned it into an organized tactic. Fighters, bombers, and even trainers were pressed into service, armed with a bomb that was never intended to be dropped and guided by pilots who were often teenaged novices with minimal flight training. Hoisington said that he was transferred from dive bombers to fighters in order to protect the ships from these *kamikazes*. Navy fighter pilots patrolled the air above the ships during the daylight hours, looking for any sign of the attackers. Difficult to stop once they were diving toward their targets, *kamikazes* often flew straight-and-level on their way to attacks, making them easier to engage. On March 27, 1945, Hoisington shot one down. He didn't want to elaborate on the details, but said it was a confirmed hit.

In addition to protecting ships from *kamikaze* attacks, Hoisington played his part in battles that are now familiar to all students of the Pacific campaign. His memoir recounted: "July 30th—Lois' birthday— We took part in a fighter sweep up at Osaka that took off at 4:30 a.m. hitting four airfields and a CVE [small carrier]."[17] Also, he wrote about bombing "Truk, the most feared Jap base in the Pacific."[18] In addition, Hoisington mentioned action over Okinawa, Tarawa, Makin, and Wake Island, as well as mainland Japan.

The men in the film appear to be very attached to each other and show sadness but not great emotion when one of their number doesn't return from a mission. Hoisington concurred with this portrayal:

> The camaraderie displayed in the movie was similar to that of the squadrons that I served in. We joked with each other probably to keep our spirits up. We lost pilots and crews but most of the time it was away from the ship. We did not see the death or pain or blood unless it was our own. That statement calls to mind the time I did see some dead men on our ship. We were on a mission to bomb a Jap battleship. While we were gone, a Kamikaze hit the *Hancock*. When we returned, the fire was out and we came aboard. After I taxied forward, I got out of the plane and went over to a hole in the flight deck. Looking down through the hole I saw men in a quad 40 mm gun mount who had their clothes burned off and whose skin was red from the blast. They lay around the mount where they had been working. My only sight of casualties.[19]

The *Commonweal* review of *Wing and a Prayer* reflected on the film's emphasis on casualties: "While I am aware that the war-weary public needs the relaxation which movie goers find in escapist comedies and melodramas, I also have a strong feeling that the public has no right to be war weary or to forget the war's issues or the suffering and sacrifices through which men are going."[20] According to this critic, *Wing and a Prayer* reminds the country that their men are dying in far-off parts of the globe, while members of the American public selfishly suffer from "war-weariness." The reviewer continued, stating that

> The best parts of *Wing and a Prayer* are the magnificent shots of the carrier, the planes landing and taking off, the movement on the deck and in the air during the battles. The film also succeeds, through its story of these clean-limbed boys, in reminding us how much we owe the young men who are actually doing the war's dirty work.[21]

These Navy pilots may have lived relatively well on board their carriers, but like all sailors they faced a hazard unique to their service: the possibility that, at any moment, an enemy torpedo or bomb could send their ship to the bottom . . . taking their home, their comrades, and all their possessions with it. Naval aviators, like generations of sailors before them, did their best to put such thoughts out of their mind, however, and focus on the work at hand. When they did—flying thousands of missions against enemy targets on land, at sea, and in the air, they played a major role in winning the war against Japan.

Overall, Hoisington agreed that *Wing and a Prayer* accurately depicts the daily life on a World War II aircraft carrier. Despite the fictionalization of the film's plot and setting, he felt that the movie provides a relatively realistic picture of his experiences on the *Enterprise*, the *Intrepid*, and the *Hancock*. He said the pilots' lives on board a carrier portrayed in the movie were pretty close to the real thing, and that viewing it brought back memories.[22]

Hoisington enjoyed his Navy days, and, following the war, he stayed in the Navy for a few years. He worked in Washington DC on rocket research, and also received advanced training at Annapolis. In 1947, a hearing problem disqualified him for the rank he desired, so he left the Navy and returned to Illinois to his family's farm, eventually pursuing a career in engineering. Hoisington attended a reunion on the *Hancock* in honor of the fiftieth anniversary of D-Day, where he was enthusiastically greeted by his former comrades as "Hose!" Every summer, he travels to Oshkosh, Wisconsin, for the Experimental Air Craft Association Fly-In, the biggest air show in the country. Whether landing on the rolling, pitching, incredibly small deck of an aircraft carrier, or just enjoying flying over the peaceful skies of central Wisconsin, Jim Hoisington has always loved airplanes and everything associated with flying them.

4

STORMY WEATHER: *MEMPHIS BELLE* AND *TWELVE O'CLOCK HIGH*

On December 7, 1941, twenty-year-old Jim Oberman was attending college in Iowa. A serious student and athlete, he had no time to see any of the Hollywood movies that dealt with the war raging in Europe and Asia, or worry about the war's implications for America's young men. He was too busy with college life to take time out to see Tyrone Power flirt and fly his way through *A Yank in the RAF* (1941), and had not heard Joel McCrea's plea to America to come to England's aid in *Foreign Correspondent* (1940). He hadn't even seen Charlie Chaplin memorably mock *The Great Dictator* (1940).

At the time, the young college student had no way of knowing that his impending military experiences and those of his comrades-in-arms would parallel the subject matter for a classic wartime documentary—*The Memphis Belle: A Story of a Flying Fortress* (1944), directed by William Wyler—as well as a fictionalized remake, *Memphis Belle* (1990), produced by Wyler's daughter Catherine. Nor did he know that he and the Eighth Air Force—which he was about to join—would also be the focus of the Hollywood classic *Twelve O'Clock High* (1950), starring Gregory Peck as Brigadier General Frank Savage, a fictionalized version of real-life Eighth Air Force Wing Commander Frank Armstrong.

Early in 1942, however, Oberman left his college campus, enlisted in the Army Air Corps, and headed for the clouds. After extensive training, the "green" B-17 captain picked up his crew and their brand-new plane, which they named *Stormy Weather* (to signify "raining" bombs on Germany, and in homage to the Lena Horne hit), and flew to Bury St. Edmunds, England, the home base from which Oberman and his crew would fly thirty-five missions over Europe.

The mission of the Eighth Air Force, of which Oberman's squadron was one small part, was to carry out high-altitude precision bombing attacks on military targets—submarine bases, railroad junctions, oil refineries, and factories producing war materiél—in Germany as well as occupied Europe. Carried out in broad daylight, these American missions complemented the night attacks on German cities carried out by heavy bombers from the Royal Air Force. The B-17 had been designed in the 1930s expressly for such a mission. With its top-secret Norden bombsight and defended by heavy machine guns, it was believed capable of dropping bombs with extraordinary accuracy while holding its own against enemy fighters. Neither expectation was entirely fulfilled in combat. High-altitude bombing, even with a high-tech bombsight, proved less efficient than prewar strategists expected, and multiple missions were often necessary to put a given target even temporarily out of action. The B-17's defensive armament, heavy as it was, proved insufficient to drive away enemy fighters, leaving the bombers vulnerable unless Allied fighters accompanied them as escorts. Until late 1943, however, no Allied fighter had sufficient range to follow B-17s deep into Germany, leaving the bombers vulnerable over the target.

Particularly in 1942 and 1943, therefore, the bomber crews of the Eighth Air Force had some of the highest casualty rates in the Allied armed forces. On one catastrophic mission against the ball-bearing factory at Schweinfurt and the Messerschmitt aircraft plant at Regensburg, sixty of the attacking B-17s were shot down by German fighters and anti-aircraft fire (which the crews, borrowing a German word, called "flak"). The Eighth's losses would have been even higher were it not for the extraordinary durability of the B-17s, which routinely limped home with engines disabled, hydraulic lines shot out, and airframes perforated with hundreds of bullet and shell holes. Many of the wounded aircraft that reached England brought dead, dying, or wounded crew members with them. Surviving a tour of duty in the Eighth—defined as twenty-five completed missions—was far from a sure thing.

After viewing both the 1944 and the 1990 versions of *Memphis Belle*, Oberman voiced his approval of William Wyler's wartime documentary, which was distributed by Paramount for the War Department and the

Office of War Information. The film takes its name from the first B-17 to complete a twenty-five-mission tour, making its crew eligible to rotate home to the United States, and follows the ten-man crew of the B-17 *Memphis Belle* on their twenty-fifth and final bombing mission. Commenting on why the *Belle* flew ten fewer missions than his own crew, Oberman said simply: "The guys who flew those earlier missions had it rougher than we did. They ran into heavier resistance."[1]

Wyler's documentary opens with a view of the peaceful, sunny English countryside. Oberman's memories differ a bit. Bury St. Edmunds may have been a tranquil English village, but the surrounding countryside had been taken over by the RAF and the United States Eighth Air Force, blanketing the landscape with airfields. And as for the climate, well, he described that as "disagreeable," rather than sunny.

In Oberman's opinion, Wyler's documentary was accurate in every other detail, from the early morning briefings to the crew's comparatively relaxed attitude on their return trip and their end-of-mission celebration. He asserts that the film parallels his own experiences flying missions over Europe. Wyler's documentary, however, clearly served War Department interests in promoting U.S. involvement in the war. The narration, written by Lester Koenig, is stirring and patriotic, and "has an almost poetic rhythm to it."[2] At one point the narrator muses, "You look at the strange world beyond—reflections in Plexiglas. Like nothing you ever saw before. Outside a dream." The ultimate goal of the narration and the film, however, is clearly to support the war effort and the bombing campaign against Germany. Elsewhere in the film, the narrator describes the enemy as "the Hun" and refers to Germans as "invaders and oppressors who twice in one generation have flooded the world with suffering . . . have brought torment and anguish, gold stars and telegrams from the War Department to American homes."[3]

To enhance its realism, the documentary intercuts this voice-over narration with sounds from inside the B-17—the drone of engines, the clatter of machine guns, and the rush of the wind through the bomb bay and the waist gunners' open windows. The audience thus hears dialogue that, though not from the mission shown, is typical of many missions.[4] Here, for example, a member of the *Belle*'s crew reports that another B-17 has been hit and, other crew members add their comments:

Come on, you guys, bail out!

How many chutes did you count?

Two. There's still eight men in that ship!

There's three more chutes!

Oberman said that such exchanges were common among his crew members. They, too, watched and waited for chutes to appear from B-17s that weren't going to make it back to England. He related how airmen kept very close track of the men who went down—"Missing, dead, prisoner of war. . . . Some downed American airmen were picked up by the French resistance and helped to escape through Spain. We accounted for every man who went down."

Wyler's striking juxtaposition of rehearsed narration and the spontaneous comments of the *Belle*'s crew is a reminder that this film was made to address a war-worn country, united in a common struggle. When a returning injured crewman receives an urgently needed blood transfusion right on the Fortress, the narrator tells his audience: "This could be the blood of a high school girl in Des Moines, a miner in Kentucky, a movie star in Hollywood, or you."[5] The wartime American audience is reminded that even though they may not be flying bombers, they can still do their patriotic duty.

A *New York Times* reviewer, commenting on the film at the time of its release, was greatly impressed with Wyler's editing, as well as the realism and drama of this "Hollywood-style" documentary:

> Perhaps the most absorbing segment of the picture is the subsequent scene showing the battle against the enemy fighters, which included dialog between the crew members on their interphones. From voices, even but tense, the audience hears—and then sees—"There's four of 'em, coming in at nine o'clock. They're breaking at eleven. Get that ball turret on 'em"—and then the angry chatter of machine guns. Or heartbreakingly, you see a giant Fortress fall dizzily off below, with black smoke billowing behind her, as a voice notes, "B-17 out of control at three o'clock"—and then follows a few moments later with an urgent appeal to stricken friends, "Come on, you guys, get out of that plane. There go three chutes. There go two more."[6]

Americans watching the *Belle*'s twenty-fifth and final mission at their local theaters were instantly transported to the lethal skies over Europe. A *Time* magazine reviewer also voiced admiration for the exciting flight:

> All of the combat shots in *The Memphis Belle* are made on the spot. . . . The hope and fear on the faces of the fliers when they get their orders to bomb Wilhelmshaven are real hope and fear. . . . The hope and anxiety of the ground crew, waiting through a long, pastoral afternoon for the plane's return are just as real. The joy of both groups when, late and limping, the *Belle* gets back loses none of its life-&-death resonance because it irresistibly suggests schoolboys and athletes when a victorious team comes home.[7]

The former schoolboys and athletes on Oberman's crew ranged from twenty to twenty-two years old. As promotional material for Catherine Wyler's later feature-length remake reminded, these "boys were asked to become men and then these men were asked to become heroes."

On four different occasions, Oberman sat in early morning briefings and learned that he and his crew were going to "Big B"—Berlin. The fear on his face and the faces of the other men assigned to bomb the Third Reich's capital city easily rivaled that on the faces of the cinematic airmen bound for Wilhelmshaven. The thought of invading skies over the heavily fortified capital was terrifying: "Berlin was very well protected by anti-aircraft guns." As Oberman noted, pilots and crews of the bombers knew only too well that it was the flak from these guns that brought down the majority of B-17s.

Faced with such challenges, bomber crewmen took every opportunity to improve their chances of coming home safely. When questioned about a scene in *The Memphis Belle* (repeated in the 1990 remake) that depicts the crew praying together before taking off, Oberman confirmed that it was not a Hollywood invention, but a reflection of reality. "We saw a lot of planes go down," he explained. "We saw lots of our friends get injured or killed. Some ships didn't make it back. Sure we prayed." The 1990 version of the film that shows several members of the crew wearing talismans, carrying good luck charms, and being exceptionally superstitious also rang true for Oberman, who commented: "Yeah, there was a lot of that, too." Crewmen in both versions of *Memphis Belle* kiss the ground on their final return to England, in scenes that struck Oberman as not merely credible, but highly authentic. He and his crew celebrated their thirty-fifth and final mission with enthusiasm and reverence, and while the aircraft commander in the 1990 version of *Memphis Belle* celebrates by dousing his crew with champagne, Oberman remembered that he and his crew celebrated with a special bottle of whiskey that they had been saving for this most special occasion.

After successfully completing their twenty-fifth mission, the crew of the *Memphis Belle* is visited by King George VI and Queen Elizabeth of England, who shake hands all around. The camera shows a nervous but beaming crewman: "Johnny Quinlan never expected anything like this to happen when he left Yonkers." The British monarchs chat with the American airman—George VI wearing the uniform of a Marshall of the Royal Air Force—while "God Save the King" is played in the background. This scene both underscores Britain's gratitude and reinforces the Anglo-American partnership. The documentary concludes with talk of ending the war that at the same time articulates the principle behind the strategic bombing campaign: that destroying the enemy's ability to fight will, inevitably, also destroy their will to fight. "Bomb the enemy again, and again, and again until he's had enough, and then we can all go home."[8] By the time the documentary was released in April 1944, the Allies were planning the invasion of Europe, and thoughts of ending the war were on everyone's mind.

The film's dramatic narration perfectly complements Wyler's cinematography. His photographic techniques for the film were groundbreaking and heralded some aspects of the cinema verité, or "reality cinema," such as handheld cameras and an emphasis on recording unmediated experience. Three different cameras filmed the sequence during *Belle*'s final mission, and one cameraman, Harold Tonnenbaum, was killed in the process.[9]

Newsweek lauded Wyler's film as "far and away one of the finest documentary films to emerge from the war on any front."[10] The reviewer continued: "The film is a blow-by-blow description of that final mission—the bombing of Wilhelmshaven's docks and submarine pens. . . . Aesthetically this Technicolor report to the nation is a thing of beauty and electrifying drama."[11] The review also reported that President Roosevelt wanted *The Memphis Belle* to be seen by everyone in the country. In a footnote, the writer added that two-time Academy Award–winner Wyler was promoted to Lieutenant Colonel and awarded the Air Medal, as well as a citation for his work on the film.

Although William Wyler's wartime documentary received Oberman's enthusiastic endorsement for its authenticity and realism, he was less impressed with Catherine Wyler's 1990 fictionalized remake. He felt that her film was too dramatic, too "Hollywood," and noted that every possible catastrophe that could befall a B-17 and its crew happened to Ms. Wyler's *Memphis Belle* during its fictitious final flight. Enemy fire riddles the plane: opening a huge hole in the fuselage, tearing a chunk out of the tail, and damaging the landing gear. The lead aircraft in the squadron is forced to drop out of formation, leaving the *Belle* to take responsibility for locating and accurately bombing the target—which turns out to be obscured by smoke. The radioman is wounded, forcing the bombardier (who completed only two weeks of medical school before dropping out to enlist) to improvise life-saving treatment. An engine catches fire, forcing the pilots to put the plane into a steep dive in order to blow the flames out. Even their return to base becomes a challenge, with the crew struggling to force the damaged landing gear into place in time. Oberman conceded that, although it was possible for all of those disasters to occur, it stretched the imagination to suggest that they would happen during a single mission. Still, he admitted, "for a movie like that, it wasn't too bad."

The film's commercialism, along with the filmmaker's attempts to create "dramatic interest" above and beyond the war, were Oberman's main qualms with the later version of *Memphis Belle*. Both prompted significant departures from reality, as he experienced it—departures that were particularly striking in the relationship between the pilot and his copilot. In the film, the easygoing copilot is at odds with the stiff, no-nonsense captain, and jealous of his command of the crew. Oberman countered that the *real* military was about effective teamwork: "I depended on my copilot completely, and he depended on me. We complemented each other to complete a joint effort; our goal was to be the best two pilots in the Eighth Air Force."

In contrast, civilian reviewers praised the film's capturing of "reality." Richard Schickel deemed this fictional version of the story of the *Memphis Belle* as real, gritty, and almost epic, claiming that the film

> displays the same virtues and flaws of her father's work. Despite the passage of a demythifying half century, this well-cast plane's crew . . . remains as wartime Hollywood insisted on imagining it . . . setting aside their small, usually comical differences to form a unit that, in

both efficiency and common decency, no tyranny could hope to beat. . . . Yet once the *Belle* is airborne, it is hard to think of a movie that has more vividly portrayed the sheer terror of being in a big tin can as it is kicked through the skies by flak and assaulted by swarms of fighters. In this, its better half, *Memphis Belle* achieves something like epic proportions. Out of an authentic emotion—fear—it finally forges the kind of unshakable link with an audience that the sweet, stale clichés of male bonding could never sustain.[12]

Newsweek's review of the 1990 fictionalized version of the *Belle*'s last mission also praised the seemingly real and terrifying flight. The reviewer applauded the "breathless hour in the air as the bomber heads toward Bremen. . . . Yet rarely—and this is its saving grace—has the sheer terror of these missions been so viscerally dramatized," citing the film as a "blunt reminder of war's bloody cost."[13] Similarly, *Film Comment* found much to admire in the fictional *Belle*:

> The movie makes us acquainted with, in fact intimate with, exactly what goes on in a Boeing B-17 with its four engines, seven machine-gun posts, and 30 tons of fully loaded weight. We see what each of the guys does; every inch of the plane and every demanding live-or-die instant of poised attention by the ten men is impressed in full urgency.[14]

Film Comment reviewer Donald Lyons argued that Catherine Wyler's film never glorifies war, but instead shows the human cost and sacrifice that war exacts:

> *Memphis Belle* neither intends or achieves bellicosity. Its final dedication is to all the brave young men, whatever their nationality, who died in the skies over Europe. . . . It was the hard fate of youngsters a long generation ago to have to witness and confront evil in Europe. . . . The final voyage of the *Memphis Belle* has yielded one of the greatest of war movies, and "Let's do it again" is certainly *not* one's feeling as the wounded plane lurches onto the softly welcoming English soil.[15]

Thus, while in 1943 William Wyler employed the real *Memphis Belle* to produce a film that implied, *We didn't start this war, but we must, we will, win it*, nearly fifty years later Catherine Wyler used that same story to suggest, *Let's enjoy our hard-won peace and war no more*—the sentiments of a younger generation as it approached the millennium.

Another Hollywood war film about which Oberman was very enthusiastic was *Twelve O'Clock High* (1949); noting that it is "the only movie about the Eighth Air Force." The film, directed by Henry King and starring Gregory Peck, Gary Merrill, and Dean Jagger (who won an Academy Award for his performance), is a quintessential Hollywood picture, but Eighth Air Force insiders such as Oberman know that it is based on the actual, real-life story of a commander—General Frank Armstrong—trying to turn around an air group that, in Oberman's words, "wasn't doing as well as it should."

As John Correll notes in *Air Force Magazine*, the film "had an authenticity seldom seen in war movies. It pushed all the right buttons for airmen, who held it in such regard that the movie became something of a cult film for generations of Air Force members."[16] Correll affirms:

Figure 4.1. *Twelve O'Clock High*: the story of the Eighth Air Force Division.

Very little of it was pure fiction. The film was adapted from a novel by Beirne Lay, Jr., and Sy Bartlett, who drew deeply on their own wartime experiences. Both had been Hollywood screenwriters before the war, but in 1943, when *Twelve O'Clock High* takes place, they were Air Force officers in England. [17]

Lay, the principal author, was either a direct participant in or an eyewitness to the main events in the story, and although the film "took some creative license in time shifting and combinations of events," it relied extensively on U.S. and German combat film footage as background for the air battles. [18]

Prior to the film's production, Air Force officials studied the *Twelve O'Clock High* script in order to identify any potential concerns. Surprisingly, the complaints and desired changes were few. [19] According to a *Time* magazine review,

> *Twelve O'Clock High* has the uncommon merit of restraint. It avoids such cinemilitary booby traps as self-conscious heroics, overwrought battle scenes and the women left behind or picked up along the way. . . . The picture concentrates on an engrossing human crisis posed by the demands of the early air war's "maximum effort." [20]

The film's invitation-only premiere at New York City's Roxy Theater was cosponsored by the U.S. Air Force and featured an opening parade of soldiers, veterans, Red Cross workers, and the Mitchell Field Air Force Band. Fifteen hundred present and former members of the Eighth Air Force were on hand for the film's opening night, including six Medal of Honor winners. After attending the premiere, even General Curtis LeMay bestowed high marks on the film: "I didn't see one technical error in this thing." [21]

The Air Force's pride in, and effusive praise for, the Hollywood film had a political dimension as well as an aesthetic one. The Air Force had become an independent branch of the armed forces—separate from and equal in stature to the Army—only three years earlier, in 1947, and was struggling to establish an identity and a clearly defined mission for itself as America's long-range striking force. Land-based heavy bombers, controlled by the newly formed Strategic Air Command (SAC), were central to that mission, and the Air Force went out of its way to promote books, articles, and films that extolled their value. *Twelve O'Clock High* fitted perfectly into that mission. The film celebrated not only the power of long-range bombing to defeat foreign enemies, but also the courage and dedication of the bomber crews who had played a major role in defeating Nazi Germany. The film's story of a tough but compassionate leader transforming the men under him into disciplined professionals matched LeMay's vision of his own role as the first commander of SAC.

Even though it tacitly endorses the power and military value of strategic bombing, *Twelve O'Clock High* is, equally, about the toll it takes on the bomber crews. A *Time* magazine critic summed up its central plot as the story of a new commander who must rebuild the morale of a bomber group whose heavy losses threaten to "1) discredit precision daylight bombing and 2) undermine the whole aerial offensive against German-held Europe."[22] The airmen in the film have seen a lot of action and many casualties; morale is at an all-time low. There is continual discussion among them about the wisdom of continuing to attempt precision bombing in daylight, unprotected by fighters and fully visible to both antiaircraft gunners on the ground and enemy fighters in the air. In the film, the most decorated man in the unit voices to his commander his uncertainty as to the prudence and effectiveness of this tactic, which mirrored Oberman's own wartime experiences. The real-life debates about the practicality of bombing by day—particularly when both the British and German air forces had abandoned the practice by 1941—were never-ending, and according to Oberman, the tactical merit was "questioned by a lot of people, from Churchill on down."

The casualty toll that daylight bombing takes, and the stress it imposes on bomber crews, inflict emotional trauma on the characters in *Twelve O'Clock High*, and the 918th Bomb Group deteriorates to the point where it cannot function. This look at the psychological expense of war was unique, and Ivan Butler considered the film a "caustic comment on the essential vileness of the war mentality."[23] The original commander of the 918th, Colonel Keith Davenport (Gary Merrill), has to be replaced by a hard-line commanding officer dispatched from headquarters, Brigadier General Frank Savage (Gregory Peck), because he has become too attached to the men he commands and is reluctant to order them into harm's way time and time again, thus risking their lives for a practice that he suspects is not worth what it costs in equipment and lives.

Savage initially presents himself as Davenport's polar opposite. His first act upon entering the 918th's base at Archbury is to chew out the guard at the gate, who fails to ask him for his credentials, and he continues to behave in a fashion that makes his men think he is cold, uncaring, and inhuman. He insists on refresher training for the group's crews, and orders tight formations and constant vigilance in the air. The pilots rebel against his hard-nosed tactics and apply, en masse, for transfers to other units, but later change their minds when the 918th, led by Savage, is the only group to return from a dangerous mission having hit the target and lost no aircraft. As the 918th begin to exhibit a newfound attitude of professionalism and unit pride, Savage allows himself to become closer to his men and gentler in handling them. Despite warnings from Davenport, the man he replaced, he comes to know his men too well; they become his friends, and the prospect of sending them on missions that they may not survive begins to tear him apart. Eventually the strain of command is more than he can take, and he breaks down.

The script originally depicted Savage's disintegration as a complete mental breakdown. However, the Air Force felt such an absolute breakdown would not be characteristic of a man who had achieved such a high rank in the military. The Air Force preferred that his collapse manifest itself in some physical manner, and the scriptwriter complied by showing Peck lying comatose in his bunk as he waits for the group to return from a mission, relaxing and sinking into a peaceful sleep only when he knows they are safe. The Air Force also objected to the portrayal of heavy whiskey drinking by American military men, so that, too, was altered. But as Oberman recalled, "whiskey was always available." When he and his fellow airmen returned from a mission, before the debriefing, they were given "whiskey, donuts, and cocoa." However, when there was a "live mission, a red light would go on in the officers' club to indicate that there should be no drinking."

In real life, as well as in the film, medical personnel watched the men closely for signs of stress and hints (like excessive alcohol consumption) that they might not be able to perform their jobs in the air. Oberman noted that on two different occasions, he and his crew were given mandatory rests and sent to a stately manor house for "R and R" to recuperate from the strains of battle.

Even with such precautions, crew members were occasionally compromised by the stress of being at war. Oberman recalled an occasion when a member of his crew could not execute his duty during a mission. B-17s were not pressurized, and above 10,000 feet oxygen masks were necessary for the crew members. Because a man could quickly die without his mask, Oberman continually checked his crew to make sure their masks were in place and functioning properly—"Navigator, oxygen check," "Navigator, oxygen ok," and so on. Once while they were under attack, Oberman called the tail gunner who did not respond, having passed out from lack of oxygen. He ordered one of the waist gunners to go to the aid of the tail gunner, but "the waist gunner lost control of himself. He couldn't do it." At that point, another member of the crew requested permission to leave his post and aid the unconscious man. Oberman gave permission, and "the life of the tail gunner was saved." However, the defense of the ship was jeopardized when one man had to leave his post and perform the duty of another. As soon as *Stormy Weather* landed in England, the crew voted unanimously to drop the waist gunner from their crew: "There was no place on a B-17 for a man who couldn't do his job."

Oberman, however, continuously praised the training that he and the other airmen received from the Army Air Forces. They were drilled for every possible situation they could find themselves in, and they depended on the other men in their crew to be just as well trained: "We all counted on each other to do our own jobs. Every man was well trained in his own job." The same virtue was highlighted by both versions of *Memphis Belle* and by *Twelve O'Clock High*, all of which show the members of bomber crews working together as members of a seamless, smoothly functioning team of specialists.

Like the B-17s in *Twelve O'Clock High*, *Stormy Weather* proved extremely durable, continuing to fly even after taking incredible abuse from enemy flak and fighters: "After one mission, we counted 150 holes in her," said Oberman. According to Oberman, the Luftwaffe wasn't as lethal as the antiaircraft guns. The flak could be so heavy on some missions that "you could walk across the sky on the puffs of smoke. The flak was that thick." Staying in formation was the B-17s' best defense. Any damaged plane that was forced to fall out of the formation was an easy target for enemy Messerschmitts. However, as the war continued, the caliber of the German fighter pilots decreased. According to Oberman, the German air force had lost too many experienced pilots, and, unlike the American rookies who were exceedingly well trained, these later German fighter pilots were not adequately prepared for combat; they often got themselves into "dumb situations" to which qualified, skilled pilots would never have fallen victim.

The Air Force believed that *Twelve O'Clock High* would serve as good public relations material, and it cooperated completely with the film's production. Officials offered the director all of the stock combat footage that he would possibly need, and deemed that enough time had passed that Americans could now be made aware of the terrible burden and stress that those in command had experienced during the war. According to Lawrence Suid in *Guts and Glory*, "The focus on one man's psychological as well as physical struggle to survive lifted *Twelve O'Clock High* out of the category of war films to the level of those few movies that make a significant comment on the human condition."[24]

Oberman effusively praised the film, claiming it was true to the minutest detail. When asked about the pressures he faced while in command, he simply responded, "That was my job." The tough life-and-death decisions he had to make concerning not only himself, but the other nine men on his ship, were now his reponsibility.

The former B-17 captain recognized that some men handled the pressure better than others, but everyone experienced some degree of stress. Although Oberman was an athlete and had never smoked prior to his time in the service, he started to smoke during the war: "It was nerves." And although his combat experiences never caused major problems for him, Oberman, like millions of other vets, has occasionally had nightmares about being in combat. "Even now, more than fifty years later, I might have a nightmare. Some guys had it a lot worse." The nightmares that Oberman suffered, however, did not extend to the damage his bombs did when they landed. In the 1990 *Memphis Belle*, the pilot is very conscious that he and his crew are dropping bombs in the vicinity of schools and other civilian-occupied buildings, and worries about the consequences of missing the intended target. Like those of most bomber pilots, however, Oberman's thoughts were focused elsewhere:

> Of course, we knew that people would be killed. But that was not our main purpose; we didn't want to kill people. Our main purpose was to destroy the German fighting machine, destroy the German military and end the war. We couldn't think about killing people. I had to think about destroying the German war machine. We didn't start the war.

Even though it is set in 1942, only seven years before it was released, *Twelve O'Clock High* opens with a trip back in time. A balding, bespectacled American bicycles into the English countryside and stops at the edge of a decommissioned wartime airfield. The hangars are empty, the runways choked with weeds, and the bombers long since gone, but the visitor's mind drifts back in time to a time when the field was active and he was stationed there. The base is Archbury, former home of the 918th, and the visitor is Savage's former adjutant, Major Harvey Stovall. As he stands beside the runway, lost in his memories, the roar of engines rises on the sound track and a B-17 swoops low over the field, preparing to land. The scene shifts to 1942, and the main story begins.

Jim Oberman has visited England several times in the decades since he completed his thirty-fifth mission. He played a part in arranging to have a memorial erected in the rose garden of Bury St. Edmunds Abbey, honoring the men of the 94th Bomber Group who gave their lives during the war. This memorial is perpetually endowed so that it will never become a burden to our British allies. Here in the United States where, as Oberman notes, the Eighth Air Force was established, a memorial was dedicated in May 1996 by Oberman and several other veterans of the air war against Germany: "It doesn't glorify war. It teaches kids that they should do everything possible to prevent war."

After V-J Day, Oberman left the Air Force and "was back in college in time to play ball in the fall." Following graduation, he married, started coaching, and raised a family. A picture of *Stormy Weather*'s crew hangs on his office wall. More than fifty years later, he has kept in touch with the men who shared life-and-death moments with him in the skies over Europe. The two *Memphis Belle* films and *Twelve O'Clock High* remain as testaments to the Eighth Air Force, and the terror experienced and bravery exhibited by the boys who "rained bombs" over Germany.

5

GUADALCANAL DIARY, BACK TO BATAAN, AND *SANDS OF IWO JIMA:* A VETERAN'S REVIEW

Today when most Americans recall the war in the Pacific, they usually think of General Douglas MacArthur, or perhaps John Wayne. In 1941 MacArthur complied with President Roosevelt's order to leave the embattled Philippines. As he left, MacArthur pledged to the Filipinos, "I shall return." The general's pledge was made good in 1944. The momentous event—MacArthur descending the ramp of a landing craft, and striding ashore through the surf—was carefully staged for newspaper and newsreel cameras. John Wayne's Pacific campaign, played out in films like *Flying Tigers* (1942), *The Fighting Seabees* (1944), and *They Were Expendable* (1945), was also just for the cameras. Those staged visual moments define the Pacific War because most of the men who served in the Pacific were never filmed doing what they did there—fighting and dying. We don't have a complete visual record of their wartime actions, but we do have Hollywood's interpretation of their combat, in films such as *Guadalcanal Diary* (1943) and *Back to Bataan* (1945). *Sands of Iwo Jima* (1949), though not released until long after the war's end, was perhaps the most influential of all. Starring John Wayne—Hollywood's version of the idealized American warrior-hero—in one of his iconic roles, it is considered by many to be the definitive film about World War II in the Pacific Theater.

Do these Hollywood films give us a picture of Pacific combat that is anywhere near realistic? On a snowy day in January 1997, Bloomington,

Illinois, native Lynn Simpson offered his views. Sitting in his comfortable living room and recalling events from fifty years before, he reviewed the thirty months he spent in combat zones in the Pacific, the entire time in close contact with enemy forces. Comparing his experiences in the Pacific to some famous Hollywood depictions of the subject—*Guadalcanal Diary* and *Back to Bataan*—he found that, although originally produced as wartime propaganda, they are surprisingly accurate depictions of what he as a young soldier encountered in the South Pacific.

Simpson was a high school senior on December 7, 1941. He had planned to attend a church-related college after graduation, and did so for a year, but then the call to arms became too strong. He forfeited his student exemption and registered for the draft. He was "called up" in March of 1943, and requested assignment to the infantry.[1] After completing basic training, Simpson was eventually assigned to Camp Roberts, California—an infantry replacement center where newly trained soldiers waited to be assigned to below-strength units. Whenever he was given leave or a pass, he would go into overcrowded, wartime San Francisco. Finding a hotel room in the city during the war was impossible, so Simpson went into all-night theaters to try to get some rest. The newsreels shown in these theaters gave the young soldier his first taste of the war, and what he saw on the screen was not very conducive to his peace of mind. The newsreels of May and June 1943 were dominated by images from the Allied campaign in North Africa. Simpson recalled that the news footage, with its images of combat and dead and wounded soldiers, impressed him tremendously.

What Simpson had yet to see in mid-1943, having spent the first year of the war in a religious college with no access to movies, were the products of Hollywood's propaganda campaign on behalf of the war. Dramatic films depicting American participation in the war began to appear in American theaters in the summer of 1942, and *Wake Island* (1942), the first of them, was "shown at training camps and military installations all over the country where it was always received with enthusiasm."[2]

These films were the product of an alliance between Hollywood and Washington, and the government created a special office to oversee the making and release of films—the Office of War Information (OWI). It was commonly known in Hollywood that the OWI viewed each new project with only one question in mind: "How will this film help us win the war?" Thus, as historian Lawrence Suid notes: "While these early movies were as always intended to make money, they were also consciously designed to lift the morale of the nation and stimulate the war effort."[3] *Wake Island*, the story of the U.S. Navy and Marines defending a strategic American holding in the Pacific in the weeks after Pearl Harbor, exemplified this strategy. It was not only a successful propaganda film—a reviewer for the *New York Times* declared that it "surely brings a surge of pride to every patriot's breast"[4]—but also showed a profit for Paramount Pictures, and garnered four Academy Award nominations.[5]

Recognizing the value of such films, the armed forces offered Hollywood their enthusiastic cooperation. *Sahara* (1943), for example, followed a lone American tank named *Lulubelle* searching for its unit in North Africa and picking up isolated soldiers—both enemy and ally—along the way.

> The army helped to create the brutal action in *Sahara* giving Columbia Pictures its full cooperation. In preparing for the production, the director, the writer, and production staff visited the Army's desert training facility in desert areas of California, Arizona and Nevada. The army provided briefings and demonstrations of tank operations . . . and donated a tank to the filmmakers for the two months the crew and actors were on location.[6]

In *Sahara*, scenes of simulated combat that Army cooperation made possible were interwoven as in *Wake Island* with a political message. The tank's commander, Sergeant Joe Gunn (Humphrey Bogart), is an American everyman: tough, resourceful, and principled. The English, French, and Sudanese soldiers that join his crew transparently represent the Allies, and the prisoners they take—a pathetic, ineffectual Italian and a sneering German—the Axis. Like *Wake Island*, the film tells the story of a small group of heroes valiantly resisting overwhelming odds—a story, in other words, designed to offer hope to Americans (both soldiers and civilians) at a time when victory was anything but certain.

Eventually, Lynn Simpson left San Francisco for Los Angeles, where he boarded a troopship bound for an unknown destination. At this point, his life began to parallel a third early Hollywood war movie: *Guadalcanal Diary*. The film, set aboard a troop-laden ship somewhere in the Pacific, was based on a best-selling book by war correspondent Richard Tregaskis. It is, as the title suggests, a semi-documentary account of the

U.S. Marines' bloody campaign to seize and hold Guadalcanal, one of the strategically vital Solomon Islands, northeast of Australia. According to Norman Kagan, the film did a good job of capturing the sense of realism: "Critics praised *Guadalcanal Diary* for the documentary feel of the invasion itself, and as one of the few films which did not use Hollywood motivations (love, bitterness, etc.), but simply had the soldiers driven by their will to survive."[7]

In the movie, the audience is immediately introduced to the "universal platoon": the New Yorker (William Bendix), the Latino (Anthony Quinn), the veteran sergeant (Lloyd Nolan), and the "kid" (Richard Jaeckel), as they wait to go ashore. The presence of Jaeckel, a teenager making his film debut, was especially appropriate since the average age of the Marines who landed on Guadalcanal was only nineteen.[8] A shipboard religious service featuring a sermon by Father Donnelly (Preston Foster)—a Notre Dame football star turned Army chaplain—draws Protestants and Jews as well as Catholics, further underscoring the diversity of the American forces.

Simpson's own platoon reflected the same all-American diversity. Although the 37th Infantry Division originally drew its members from an Ohio National Guard unit, it had been reinforced by soldiers from all over the United States. Simpson remembered young Hispanic men from Texas, young Jewish men from New York, and even a young Russian immigrant—who was eventually taken captive, beaten, and killed by the Japanese. Memories of some "Southern boys sitting around the fire and drinking some of their homemade alcohol" rounded out his memories.

In August 1943 the 37th Infantry relieved the First Marine division that is depicted in *Guadalcanal Diary*. The marines had already established a 100-yard beachhead when Simpson's division arrived to replace them in October 1943. "For the first ten to fifteen days, combat was very heavy," said Simpson. There was a great deal of sniper fire, and the island was never really secured. Eventually, however, because of casualties and lack of a more experienced candidate, Simpson himself was made a sergeant in charge of communication: "The guy in the movie running around carrying the heavy radio on his shoulder; that was me."

When asked what it was like to be in combat, Simpson replied that he really did not have time to think about it; "I had a job to do"—communication—that was his main responsibility and his biggest concern. Being in combat, in mortal danger, is almost impossible to imagine for someone who has never experienced it. However, Simpson contends that *Guadal-canal Diary* does a commendable job of re-creating the action. According to Koppes and Black in *Hollywood Goes to War*, the OWI was impressed with the combat scenes in *Guadalcanal Diary* as well:

> OWI reviewers praised the film as "the most realistic and outstanding picture" about the Pacific war they had seen. The enemy were "formidable" but not "supermen." American soldiers represented a "cross-section of the nation." The film was recommended for distribution overseas.[9]

The film's patriotic scenes were indeed convincing. In addition to the OWI's appreciation of this early war/propaganda film, "The Marine Corps recognized the importance of the film and helped in its production. The investment paid off: they set up recruiting stations near theaters showing the film and received more than twelve thousand new recruits."[10]

The film's depictions of life at the front also rang true for Simpson. He recalled his own sergeant making him a runner so that, at first, he could spend most of his time close to the sergeant at company headquarters— much as Gunnery Sergeant "Hook" Malone advises the teenaged Johnny Anderson to stay close to him in the film. Although the soldiers lived in foxholes with absolutely no comforts, they did receive their mail from home just like the Marines in the film. Regardless of where he was, Simpson always received his mail from home. Mail was not the only diversion the soldiers received from the United States: when the 37th was stationed on the island of Bougainville in the fall of 1944, they were visited by a USO troupe that included actor Randolph Scott and actor/comedian Joe E. Brown, who had lost a son in the war. Unfortunately, they didn't see any pretty American girls: "No women from the USO got that close to combat or sniper fire." According to Simpson, on Guadalcanal and Bougainville, the sniper fire was especially intense near the airfields. He likened the situation to that in the John Wayne–Robert Ryan vehicle *Flying Leathernecks* (1951), in which the pilots and the mechanics are regularly harassed by Japanese snipers.

Questioned if any scenes from *Guadalcanal Diary* didn't "ring true," Simpson singled out a scene in which Marines gathered around the radio to listen to the 1942 World Series. "I'm not saying that they didn't have a radio, but we sure didn't." In voicing this criticism, Simpson echoed a grievance shared by many other soldiers in World War II combat zones: they had no idea what was going on anywhere in the world except on the piece of ground they could see with their own eyes. The wider world—the score in the World Series, or the progress of the war—remained a mystery: "You just know your own business."

In the film, the soldiers complain about the food they are served, but Simpson had few problems with his own rations. He thought his unit's mess sergeant did a good job of getting hot meals to the soldiers when it was at all possible. He recalled that he and his fellow infantrymen took three days' worth of C-rations—canned meals built around foods like pork and beans, or meat-and-vegetable hash—into combat with them. At the end of three days, if all went according to plan, their company kitchen would be in a position to serve them hot meals again. Simpson recalled, however, being told about a time in August 1943 (before he joined his regiment) when the plans went badly wrong. The men were assigned to a roadblock near a Japanese airfield and were completely surrounded by the enemy and cut off from any other U.S. forces and supplies for forty days. Simpson reported that he and his buddies soon learned that being treated to such delicacies as fresh eggs and oranges was a definite sign that they were being readied to make yet another invasion.

After Guadalcanal, Simpson was ordered to Bougainville, the largest of the Solomon Islands, where he and his comrades-in-arms supported the Third Marine Division: "I didn't know if I was in the Army or the Marines." He spent thirteen months on Bougainville while it was classified as a combat zone. Every time his division asked to be relieved for some rest and recreation, the request was denied. According to reports, Admiral Nimitz and General MacArthur—commanders of Allied forces in the Central and Southwest Pacific, respectively—felt that the division was too far away from New Zealand or Australia to be sent there, and that it would be closer to send the men to California for some rest. In the end, they were never sent anywhere except to Bougainville: another island where the war was hot.

There, they fought for Hill 400 for three months. Simpson recalled that "during the Japanese counteroffensive, we had hand-to-hand combat." He confirmed that the hand-to-hand combat scenes portrayed in *Guadalcanal Diary* were realistic, and also recollected that counterattacks often took place at night. In January 1945, Simpson and his division left Bougainville and headed toward the Philippines. At this point, they moved into the territory depicted in the film *Back to Bataan* (1945), where—after the Japanese conquest of the Philippines in 1942—Colonel Joseph Madden (John Wayne) and Captain Andrés Bonifácio (Anthony Quinn) form native Filipinos into a guerilla army to drive out the invaders. Simpson remembers participating in a similar international partnership, noting, "I fought alongside of the remnant of the Filipino army all the way to Manila."

Directed by Edward Dmytryk, the film begins with scenes of a real-life incident: U.S. Army Rangers and Filipino guerillas liberating more than five hundred American prisoners from a Japanese prison camp near Cabanatuan in the Philippines. The film then flashes back to 1942 and recounts the history of the war in the Philippines: the surrender of the remaining U.S. forces on the Bataan Peninsula, the years of civilian resistance and guerilla warfare that followed, and the American reconquest of the islands in late 1944. The last scenes in the film return to the raid on the prison camp—less than six months in the past when the film was released on June 25, 1945, and still fresh in the minds of the audience—and the triumphant release of the prisoners. Adding to the film's sense of realism was the fact that twelve of the men shown in the final scenes actually *had* been rescued from Japanese prison camps.

The makers of *Back to Bataan* make it clear, throughout the film, that the Japanese were savage fighters, and cruel oppressors of the lands they occupied.[11] Films that demonized the enemy were nothing new, but by the time Hollywood released *Back to Bataan*, the war film had undergone some reformations and the realities of war were being portrayed:

> In the midst of its overdone action scenes, *Back to Bataan* (1945) shows the maturing of Hollywood war movies. Compared to the battle scenes in *Bataan* (1943), those in *Back to Bataan* are noticeably more realistic, conveying a strong sense of fear and pain—wounded men scream. There is also some of the introspective philosophizing that characterizes later films. The farewell, "I'll be seeing you" is used many times in the film and is made touching by frequent discussions of how in wartime people meet and then soon separate, never to meet again. Victory celebrations were accompanied by memories of the dead.[12]

Simpson remembered many incidents that took place during the U.S. invasion of the Philippines that will seem familiar to those who have seen

Back to Bataan. The first or second night on the Philippine island of Luzon was very, very dark, and a Japanese prisoner-of-war was brought to Simpson's foxhole. Since it was so dark, he could not take the prisoner back to the rear until morning. He spent the night watching the Japanese soldier, who spent the night watching him. When American and Filipino forces started advancing on Manila, they suffered severe losses, and during the Battle of Manila itself, Simpson's company had "very high casualties. The company was supposed to consist of a total of 198 men, but we were reduced to seventeen men and two officers."

On the road to Manila, Simpson also saw evidence of the Japanese cruelty dramatized in *Back to Bataan*: "Dead civilians were lying in the ditches with their hands tied behind their backs with barbed wire. They had been tortured and bayoneted." Simpson maintains that of the 100,000 civilians who died during the occupation, 80,000 were systematically executed by the Japanese. Manila had been bombarded so heavily that hardly a building was left standing. Those who remained lived in makeshift villages of shacks like the one Simpson found in a park, where some Filipinos had been living since their homes in Manila had been ravaged by the fighting. The American-Filipino army engaged in thirty days of intense combat in taking the Philippine capital. Simpson recalls, "The fighting was street-by-street once we were inside of the city."

Although the movie *Back to Bataan* ends at the point where Simpson's participation began, he affirmed that the film is a good depiction of what it was like to fight on Luzon. A contemporary reviewer for *Newsweek* agreed:

> RKO-Radio credits the Army, Navy, Marine Corps, Coast Guard and the Philippine Government with assists on *Back to Bataan*. The studio hasn't let the official collaboration down. Although the film is a regulation war picture in many ways, it is notable as . . . intelligent. [13]

A review that appeared in *The New Yorker* when *Back to Bataan* was released also found the film to be realistic: "A foreword says that this is not an invented story but what actually happened. With some reservations, having to do chiefly with a beautiful native spy, I am ready to believe that." [14] As a seasoned combat veteran who fought in the Pacific, Simpson attests that nothing in *Guadalcanal Diary* or *Back to Bataan*, including the cruelty of the Japanese occupation, violates his sense of how things actually were in the zones in which he fought. The picture of the Pacific War that these two films portray is never too fictionalized as to be unbelievable.

One notable aspect in which wartime films differ from Simpson's recollections are the names applied to the Japanese. Wartime films routinely used derogatory language, such as "All I want to do is get me a Jap. Just one Jap," in *Bataan* (1943). It was, as Bernard Dick notes in *The Star Spangled Screen*, part of "Hollywood's revilement of Japan after its 'unprovoked and dastardly attack' on Pearl Harbor . . . unparalleled in movie history."[15] Hollywood was quick to execute America's "Slap the Jap" policy, and by the spring of 1942 racial epithets were "flying fast" and routinely included in Hollywood scripts. Savage dismissals of the enemy's humanity accompanied them. In *Hollywood Goes to War*, Koppes and Black described the prevailing attitude toward the Japanese in *Guadalcanal Diary*:

> The enemy is described as apes and monkeys who hide in trees and use unfair tactics to lure unsuspecting Americans to their deaths. When [Lloyd] Nolan is asked how he feels about killing people, he replies: Well it's kill or be killed—besides they ain't people. . . . They were things to be killed, driven from the earth, according to the film's narrator.[16]

In *The Flying Tigers* (1942), for example, a character matter-of-factly states: "I hear those Japs glow in the night like bugs."[17] During the war years, the savagery woven through these wartime films was accepted as part of the attitude essential for victory. Seen today, however, it is repugnant and shocking. Simpson, whatever he or his comrades may have thought about the Japanese at the time, did not use racial epithets in recalling the war, nor did he relate any instances of racial bigotry. When recalling the war, he simply referred to the Japanese as "the enemy."

The difference between wartime and postwar attitudes shaped, in other ways, a third Pacific War film that Simpson especially admires: *Sands of Iwo Jima* (1949). He observed that after the war, when all the smoke from the fighting had cleared, it was easier to put all of the pieces together and create a war film that presented a more complete picture.[18] The film follows a U.S. Marine platoon into battle—first during the Battle of Tarawa in 1943, and later during the Battle of Iwo Jima in 1945—under the direction of the tough, relentless Sergeant John Stryker (John Wayne). Although it uses actual battles as bookends, the film is not (like the other two discussed in this chapter) primarily a re-creation of actual events. Instead, it shows the transformation of Stryker's "universal platoon" from inexperienced rookies whose careless mistakes endanger themselves and others, to a tightly bonded unit of combat veterans. The change is reflected in the men's changing attitude toward Stryker himself. Initially resentful of his harsh discipline and high expectations, they gradually come to realize that it is precisely those qualities that have turned them into effective fighters.

Producer Edmund Grainger received more extensive assistance from the military on *Sands* than he had been given for any other World War II film. The U.S. Marines assigned Captain Leonard Fribourg to serve as the film's technical advisor. His only instruction from the Marine Corps commandant was "to ensure technical veracity on the film and provide complete cooperation to the studio."[19] Captain Fribourg followed these instructions ardently and often vetoed scenes that he felt went too far afield of military practice. In fact, he "worked on the studio lot, selecting combat footage to match with the company's own battle sequences."[20] A company of genuine Marines served as background for the principal actors: "For the large assault sequences, Fribourg arranged to have the equivalent of a battalion of Marines as well as various types of equipment perform for the cameras."[21] John Wayne, the star of the film, spent several days studying a Marine warrant officer who seemed to project the same qualities as his character, Sergeant Stryker.

According to Suid, "Marine heroes David Shoup and Jim Crowe re-created their actions at the Tarawa seawall, but not until the script was rewritten—at Shoup's insistence—to portray events as they actually occurred."[22] The battle scene in the movie was so authentic and realistic that Shoup recalled "it was a fearsome thing to look at because having experienced the battle, goddamn, I didn't want to go through it again."[23] To intensify the realism, for the final sequence Grainger had Marine veteran Captain George Schrier re-create his own part in leading the patrol that raised the American flag atop Iwo Jima's Mount Suribachi—the iconic scene captured by *Life* photographer Joe Rosenthal and re-created in the U.S. Marine Corps Memorial and thousands of other places. The filmmakers' concern for detail produced a film hailed for its realism: "Other Marines later told Grainger that the film was the finest Marine Corps picture ever made by the motion picture industry . . . because it told the truth."[24]

Figure 5.1. Tough-as-nails Sergeant Stryker (John Wayne) leads his squad in the invasion of Tarawa.

Simpson agreed. He thought John Wayne portrayed the image of the American fighting man well because Wayne "looked very natural—not so glamorous as some movie stars." One equally unglamorous aspect of jungle warfare, rarely shown in the movies but suffered by Simpson and practically all who served in the Pacific, was malaria. Although nearly everyone in the South Pacific contracted the mosquito-borne illness, hardly anyone was hospitalized with it: "If all of the men who had suffered from malaria were evacuated, no one would be left to fight the war." The Army couldn't afford to lose soldiers to malaria. Simpson said that soldiers were "given atabrine to suppress the fever" and were expected to carry on with their combat duties. After meals, an officer handed out this medication to each soldier and watched the G.I. swallow it. For years after the war, Simpson continued to suffer with bouts of malaria and was regularly hospitalized as a result.

The recurrent bouts of fever, chills, and weakness associated with malaria relapses were not the only legacies of the war for veterans of the Pacific conflict. Following the war, servicemen often experienced a variety of "aftereffects," both physical and emotional, similar to those depicted in *The Best Years of Our Lives* (1946). Simpson's own period of readjustment after returning from the Pacific to Illinois paralleled that of Al Stephens, Frederic March's character in the film, and—like Stephens—he frequently celebrated his homecoming at local bars. Mrs. Simpson helped her husband relate stories of how, at approximately three o'clock in the morning, he would call his mother from a bar to tell her that he would be home "late." In an even more dramatic similarity, Dana Andrews's character in *Best Years* suffers psychological pain—what would today be identified as post-traumatic stress disorder or PTSD—and awakens in the night screaming while dreaming that he is again in combat, under attack. Simpson, according to his wife, suffered similar nightmares, and would literally jump out of bed and crawl under it if there was a loud noise outside. Because they lived near a rail yard, the combat veteran spent many restless nights taking cover under his bed.

Simpson left the Army as a sergeant, having received numerous commendations for his service. Among these are three Bronze Stars, a Good Conduct Medal, and campaign medals including the Philippines Liberation Ribbon and the Philippine Presidential Citation Badge. He keeps in touch with several old Army buddies, regularly attends reunions, and in 1995 was one of six American veterans on hand to commemorate the fiftieth anniversary of the liberation of Manila. The months that he spent in the South Pacific seem as clear and memorable to him today as they were when he returned home immediately after the war, fresh from combat and still yellow from the side effects of malaria treatment.

6

STALAG LUFT III: TALES OF
THE GREAT ESCAPE

On the day Pearl Harbor was bombed, Ernest Thorp was a student at the University of Illinois. Having seen many of the prewar films such as *The Mortal Storm* (1940), *A Yank in the RAF* (1941), and *Mrs. Miniver* (1942), he thought that any film that featured the Royal Air Force "was just great."[1] There was no doubt in his mind about the part he would play if the United States entered the war. While Thorp was still a boy, Charles Lindbergh became his all-time hero. His parents had given him a large color picture of an airborne *Spirit of St. Louis*, which, to this day, hangs on his office wall.

After Pearl Harbor, Thorp was ready to enlist, but since he was quite close to graduation the Army advised him to join the ROTC and wait to sign up until after he earned his degree. When he was one semester shy of graduation, however, the university instituted a policy that would award him his diploma if he was inducted, and Thorp immediately took the university up on its offer. He had already seen actor and real-life pilot Jimmy Stewart climb out of his plane and encourage young men in the movie audiences to join him in the defense of their country, and having earned his pilot's license as a civilian, Thorp was ready to join Stewart and the RAF in the sky.

After several months of rigorous military training, Thorp was certified as a B-17 copilot and departed for England, a country covered with airfields. Before he was able to join up with what was supposed to be his regular crew, the plane was shot down during a bombing mission. Thorp, therefore, was rotated to several different ships that required a copilot, and rarely flew with the same crew twice. By April 8, 1944, he had completed seventeen flights successfully, but according to Thorp, his eighteenth mission was "SNAFU from the very beginning." He was supposed to be sitting this mission out on a pass in London, but somehow the orders were fouled up, and he didn't get his pass for leave. At first, he viewed the error philosophically, reasoning that this mission would just put him one step closer to completing a thirty-five mission tour of duty and earning his ticket home. Almost immediately, however, the problems set in.

First, Thorp discovered that some equipment he was responsible for had been misplaced by a fellow crew member. Later on that flight, Thorp's ship was hit, and the inexperienced captain dropped out of formation. Thorp, older and more experienced even though he was copilot, took the controls. He knew that staying in formation was the B-17's best defense, and he worked to rejoin the squadron. Unfortunately, the plane had lost power in one of its four engines, and when the pilot reached for the switches that would "feather" its propeller—turning the blades edge-on to the wind in order to reduce drag—he feathered the wrong engine by mistake. Now they had just two engines, but B-17s had made it home under those conditions before, and Thorp felt that they were still "doing ok." Soon, however, another engine was hit. Even flying on just one engine, Thorp was sure they could make it back to England, but a fire broke out aboard the aircraft, and the crew knew it was a matter of seconds before it exploded. The men quickly bailed out over the North Sea.

After some time in the water (he doesn't know how long), Thorp was nearly frozen and had calmly accepted his inevitable death when he suddenly saw a German fishing boat. The German fishermen picked up Thorp and others from his crew. The captain of the boat explained that he had been a prisoner of war held in England during the Great War, and, since the British had treated him well, he would treat their American allies well in return. Although Thorp offered the fisherman money in payment for his rescue, the German refused, not wanting to be caught with Allied currency, and accepted only one British coin and a stick of gum. Thorp mused in retrospect, "I thought my life was worth more than a stick of gum."

When they arrived onshore, German soldiers were waiting to take Thorp to an interrogation center. After days of military cross-examination and solitary confinement, Thorp's interrogator shook his hand and stated: "Lieutenant Thorp, you're a good soldier. When you get to the camp, keep busy; there's plenty to do while you're there."

Thorp was transported to Stalag Luft III on a German railroad. He and the other prisoners with him knew that the railroads were a prime target for Allied bombers, so they prayed they would not be bombed by their own air forces. When he finally arrived safely, Thorp found approximately 1200 British RAF officers and about 400 American Army Air Forces officers imprisoned in the camp, which was run by the Luftwaffe—the camp was an all air force affair.

He soon noticed that the men, particularly the British, were wearing black cloth triangles on their sleeves. It was explained to him that the triangles were in memory of "the blokes who were shot," and Thorp immediately realized that he was in the camp from which the "Great Escape" had taken place. He was well aware of the details of the Great Escape, as the news of seventy-six men tunneling out of a German prisoner-of-war camp in 1944 had made newspaper headlines all over England. In 1963, this very same "Great Escape" would serve as inspiration for a big-budget American movie filmed on location, in what was then West Germany. Thorp is well acquainted with this film, and he compared his own experiences in Stalag Luft III with those depicted in the movie.

The Great Escape, directed by John Sturges, is based on the book of the same name by Paul Brickhill. A veteran of the RAF and a former Stalag Luft III prisoner himself, Brickhill had played a minor role in the escape by acting as a "stooge"—one of those tasked with watching German guards and warning fellow members of the escape organization if they got too close to a sensitive area. Brickhill remarks, in the introduction to the book, that after reading the manuscript his wife asked him, "Is it true?" and he responded, "Yes, it's all true."[2] The film makes a similar claim of authenticity. At the very beginning, a statement appears on the screen informing the viewer that "every detail of the escape is the way it really happened." Thorp can verify the truth of this claim. He lived in a room with six other men, and some of them had been scheduled to make the escape, but the plan was foiled before their numbers came up. He also heard stories about the tunnels that were dug under the campgrounds. He was in the prison for about a month, however, before anyone really confided in him. The other prisoners needed to make sure that he was not a plant—a German who spoke excellent English and was capable of passing as an American—sent into the camp to spy on the prisoners and report to the guards, as Sergeant Frank Price (Peter Graves) does in the play-turned-film *Stalag 17* (1953). Once he passed his "test," however, Thorp was assigned to watch the "ferrets"—a special subgroup of German guards, identifiable by their black coveralls, who poked around the camp looking for signs of dirt from tunnels and other evidence that the prisoners were up to something.

Soon after his arrival, Thorp was integrated into camp life. The British, some of whom had been prisoners since the fall of France in May 1940, had the place very well organized. Captured officers, according to the Geneva Convention, could not be made to work, so they needed to do something to occupy their time. One feature immediately noticeable in *The Great Escape* is the relative comfort in which the prisoners passed their time. Thorp reported that the British fashioned a soccer field in the camp, as well as a cricket field. They had even laid out a three- or four-hole primitive golf course. The prisoners had a library, and also instituted classes in which prisoners who were experts in a particular field would instruct others. Thorp himself had started a class in German when the camp had to be suddenly evacuated due to the Russian army's advancement into Germany. According to Thorp there were no pinup girls or pictures of sweethearts adorning the barrack walls, but there were art contests in which the best artistic rendering of a beautiful girl was acclaimed. The Brits also received special books for keeping diaries during their incarceration, and Thorp was given one so that he could record his time in Stalag Luft III.

Many of the prisoners in Stalag Luft III channeled their energy and leisure time into planning and executing escapes. Many of them, in Thorp's experience as well as in the film, saw escape attempts as part of their duty as officers. It was not only a matter of pride—in the film Squadron Leader Roger Bartlett (Richard Attenborough), the mastermind behind the Great Escape, declares that "it would be humiliating to knuckle under and crawl"—but a way of continuing the war. Thorp explained that the British, especially, felt the need to continue to be contributing soldiers. British officers saw escaping as their military and patriotic duty, since it would divert many Germans from the warfront in order to search for and attempt to apprehend escaped allies. Many of the British prisoners had been in the camp for years without any reliable war information. The recently arrived American airmen realized that the allies were winning the war and it was only a matter of time.

Stalag Luft III represented a particular challenge because it had been designed specifically to thwart escape attempts. The barracks were raised off the ground on brick pillars in order to create open space beneath and make it harder for allies to dig tunnels underneath without detection. Microphones buried under the surface of the compound allowed the Germans to listen for the telltale sounds of digging, and the gray dirt that covered the parade ground made the sandy, yellowish soil that tunneling would produce difficult to conceal. Barbed-wire fences patrolled by guards and watched over by towers with searchlights and machine guns ringed the camp, and any prisoner venturing too close—into an off-limits zone marked by a calf-high "warning wire"—was liable to be shot without warning. Beyond the fence, the surrounding forests had been felled by Russian prisoners held in a nearby camp, leaving would-be escapees little cover.

The premise of *The Great Escape* is that the Luftwaffe, having built a theoretically "escape-proof" camp, proceeds to transfer all of its most escape-prone prisoners there—to, as the German commandant says, "put all its rotten eggs in one basket." Recognizing one another from previous camps, the veteran escape artists quickly form themselves into what they call the "X Organization": a core group of twelve to fifteen experts in various escape-related specialties—forgery, tailoring, tunneling, surveying, diversions—each of whom, in turn, directs the efforts of a network of assistants and accomplices spread throughout the camp. Realizing that the Luftwaffe have put virtually every escape expert in Germany at his disposal, Bartlett—the head of the organization—proposes that they dream big: dig three tunnels (code-named Tom, Dick, and Harry) simultaneously, produce escape equipment in mass quantities, and eventually break out 250 men in a single night.

The film unfolds as a series of scenes showing how Bartlett and his team meet and overcome the unique challenges of breaking out of Stalag Luft III. When the night of the escape arrives, the 250 men chosen for the breakout—picked by lottery from the many hundreds who worked to make it possible—have each been supplied with clothes, food, compasses, and forged travel documents, allowing them to pass as Germans or foreign guest workers. They pass through a tunnel lit by stolen electric

Figure 6.1. Robert Strauss, William Holden, and Harvey Lembeck in *Stalag 17* (1953), a fictional depiction of life in a Luftwaffe POW camp.

lights and equipped with small wheeled platforms that roll on wooden rails—speeding their passage and preventing dirt stains on their clothes. The X Organization's collective ingenuity bests the Germans, but in the end is undone by chance events that throw off the timetable, causing the escape to be discovered after less than a third of the planned 250 men have made it out. Of the seventy-six who get away, only three (as in real life) reach freedom. The remainder are recaptured, and fifty are taken by the Gestapo to an open field where they are executed—cut down by machine guns—as a warning to others. The story ends with a title card declaring, "This film is dedicated to the Fifty."

The seventy-six men who actually made the Great Escape accomplished precisely what Roger Bartlett (whose real-life counterpart was named Roger Bushell) had hoped: five million German soldiers and policemen participated in some manner in hunting and recapturing seventy-three of the escapees. Unfortunately, the film doesn't give the impression that such a massive number of Germans were employed in the vast manhunt. According to a July 1963 *Newsweek* review,

> The search also begins to suggest that the Germans may have been discommoded—but no one would guess from seeing the movie that five million of them were occupied in the hunt, that the process of decision making and the hierarchies of command were seriously shaken by 76 men. That is the whole point of the story, the exemplary greatness of the escape—and the film scarcely touches on it. Sturges has made *The Magnificent Seven* over again, with a new locale. The 76 really were magnificent—and Sturges should have shown how and why.[3]

Thorp revealed additional details about the Great Escape that were not included in the movie. While the story line implies that after their recapture, those chosen to be executed were simply selected at random, Thorp disclosed that the condemned men were carefully chosen by the Germans. The men who were perceived to be the leaders, who spoke deceptively fluent German, and who had attempted several previous escapes were the ones designated to be shot.

Thorp also related that Hitler wanted to execute *all* the recaptured men, but the Nazi hierarchy, who feared Allied retaliation on German prisoners-of-war, dissuaded him. The film also overlooks the fact that, even though all but three escapees were recaptured and fifty of those recaptured were shot, the Great Escape was nevertheless considered a moral victory for all of those incarcerated by the Nazis: "The escape had special significance because it revealed a woeful inability on the part of the Third Reich to deal with whole men."[4]

The Great Escape, like many World War II films of the 1960s, included a large cast of established and rising stars. Most of them, however, played characters who were defined as much by their roles in the escape organization as by their personalities. James Coburn, for example, played "the Manufacturer," whose specialty was using scavenged materials to create vital pieces of equipment like an air pump to ventilate the tunnels. Charles Bronson—who, like Coburn, had worked with Sturges on *The Magnificent Seven* (1960)—was "the Tunnel King," whose skill and fearlessness as an excavator belied his fear of enclosed spaces. David McCallum, a year away from achieving international stardom as Ilya Kuryakin on the television series *The Man from U.N.C.L.E.*, played the officer in charge of "Dispersal": the problem of disposing of yellowish dirt from the tunnels in a compound whose surface was gray dust.

The one conspicuous exception to the pattern was Captain Virgil Hilts, whose nickname, "the Cooler King," referred not to his "job" but to his history of rule-breaking and stints in the camp's solitary confinement cells ("the cooler"). Steve McQueen, who played Hilts, was the biggest star in *The Great Escape*, familiar to American audiences from *The Magnificent Seven* and the western television series *Wanted: Dead or Alive*. He is the centerpiece of several of the film's most clearly invented (or embellished) scenes: clowning with two other American prisoners on the Fourth of July, knocking down a German guard who is about to shoot a fellow prisoner, and playing catch with himself—bouncing a baseball off the concrete walls of the cooler—in order to pass the time in solitary. He is also featured in the film's biggest action sequence: racing for the Swiss border on a hijacked Wehrmacht motorcycle, and attempting (unsuccessfully) to jump the barbed-wire barrier that lies between him and freedom.

McQueen's portrayal of Hilts was Thorp's only major complaint with *The Great Escape*. According to Thorp, the Germans had a number of rules and regulations that were nonnegotiable, and McQueen's character frequently violated these rules and also directly or indirectly insulted the Germans. "He never would have gotten away with his attitude." The former POW explained that "you never talked back, and he would not have been allowed a ball and glove." *Newsweek* also found fault with McQueen:

> Steve McQueen . . . is too sardonic, too cute, too irrepressible to be believed. Like a show-off kid in the third grade, he is forever up to little pranks, getting himself thrown into solitary confinement, where he bounces a baseball off the wall as if he were confined in a playground.[5]

Even though Steve McQueen looks and acts too much like a 1960s-style rebel-with-a-motorcycle to be believable as a 1940s soldier, in *War Movies*, Jay Hyams concedes that "the film's most spectacular scenes are of McQueen trying to jump a motorcycle over a barricade on the Swiss border."[6] Norman Kagan agreed: "Steve McQueen on his getaway motorcycle made an exhilarating figure of fun and freedom."[7] He represents the "spirit" of the Great Escape—the defiance, tenacity, and inventiveness of the escapers—made a bit more tangible and exciting for moviegoers.

Although McQueen's character hit a false note with Thorp, Hilts's on-screen buddy, Scottish ex-jockey Archie Ives (Angus Lennie) was a recognizable camp personality to Thorp. Ives, having been behind the wire for years, grows increasingly desperate for freedom, and willing to take enormous risks to obtain it. He first enlists Hilts in a scheme to "blitz out": that is, to make a risky escape attempt with a short timetable, minimal preparation, and thus little chance of being discovered in advance. The pair, he explains, will tunnel under the wire like moles: one behind the other, one clawing the loose, sandy soil out of their path and pushing it backward to the other, who packs it behind them. When this attempt fails, landing them both in the cooler and turning Ives increasingly desperate, Hilts urges him to hang on and wait for a chance to go out through the X Organization's primary tunnel: Tom. This temporarily calms the Scotsman, but when the Germans discover Tom, Ives snaps and—with a faraway look in his eyes—runs for the wire and tries to climb it. Thorp recalled incidents where men went mad and just ran toward the barbed wire in an attempt to get out. They were, like Ives, immediately shot by the guards. Thorp said, "The Brits called it 'going around the bend.'"

Thorp also revealed that the prisoners never used the words "escape" or "tunnel." These words were verboten—forbidden, lest they be overheard and tip off the ferrets to an escape in progress. An "escape committee" monitored all ongoing escape attempts, and if a man was planning to break out, he had to obtain its approval before going forward, lest his actions interfere with or endanger others already under way. Very few people in the camp actually knew who was on the escape committee; a would-be escapee started inquiries at a very low level and eventually might get an audience with the escape committee itself. In the film, the committee is represented by Bartlett (Big X) and the X Organization's chief of security, MacDonald (Gordon Jackson). McQueen goes before them to obtain authorization for his "mole" blitz-out with Ives, and the committee—though astonished by the mad simplicity of the plan—ultimately approves it in the interest of keeping up normal appearances in the camp. If *all* escape attempts suddenly cease, Bartlett reasons, the Germans will begin to wonder what their escape-minded captives are up to.

The escape committee's use of Hilts and Ives's attempted blitz-out as a decoy reflects its concern with the "long game." So, too, does a second, less formal meeting between Hilts, Bartlett, and MacDonald. Desperate for intelligence about the territory between the camp and the nearby town,

Big X asks Hilts if he would be willing to break out—taking advantage of a blind spot between the guard towers where a single man could cut through the wire unnoticed—in order to survey the area. When he is recaptured, Bartlett reasons, he will carry the vital intelligence back to camp with him. Hilts, realizing that the plan requires him to *let* himself be recaptured even if he could have gotten away, angrily declines. He changes his mind, however, after his buddy Ives is shot to death on the wire. "I'm going out tonight," he tells Bartlett quietly, doing what every member of the real-life X Organization did: temporarily set aside his individual desire for freedom in order to work on a scheme that would bring freedom to many.

Because the Germans had recently shot the fifty recaptured escapees, most of the Americans imprisoned with Thorp, convinced that the fighting would soon be over, were satisfied to spend the rest of the war biding their time in camp. Even so, Thorp affirmed, the conditions under which he and the other men lived meant that escape was still entirely possible. The second major action scene at the climax of *The Great Escape*— American pilot Bob Hendley (James Garner) and a buddy stealing a German airplane and trying to fly it to Switzerland—was, Thorp explained, not all that far-fetched. Indeed, a similar event actually happened. The Luftwaffe routinely allowed Allied pilots to fly German planes—"of course, they didn't have much gas and they did have a fighter escort." The prisoners agreed that this was all strategic: the Germans were hoping that the Allied pilots, happy to be back in the air and around fellow aviators, would relax and divulge information about Allied aircraft that would be useful to German engineers.

Although Thorp's assignment was security, he was well aware that there were prisoners in camp who were master scroungers, master forgers, and master engineers. In discussing the intricate process depicted in one scene of the film in which blankets and old remnants of cloth are styled into civilian suits, counterfeit German uniforms, and workmen's clothes, Thorp proudly declared that they had "excellent tailors in camp." The men of Stalag Luft III also produced forged papers, including photos and passports, and created assembly lines to turn out escape rations and tiny compasses. Thorp explained that a great deal of bribery went on within the camp, and practically anything could be obtained if the price was right. Similarly, in the film, the imagination and resourcefulness

Figure 6.2. Former pilot Ernest Thorp, with a model of Stalag Luft III—where he was held prisoner—the site of the real-life "Great Escape."

demonstrated by the British and some American officers would put the Swiss Family Robinson to shame. A film review in *Time* reported:

> Every plotter does his part. To the sound of a tunnel being chipped through the concrete floor of a bunk house washroom, the clink of the pick hammer is synchronized with the banging of the hammer innocently driving a horse-shoe pitching stake outside. Wardrobes of German clothes are being run up from blankets and uniforms dyed in coffee or ink; whole wallets full of identification papers are forged; money, emergency rations, maps are scrounged. [8]

In the film, Hendley's role in the organization is "the Scrounger"—the man who, one way or another, can procure any item his campmates need, from steel bars to make pickaxes for tunnel crews ("liberated" from the suspension of a supply wagon parked outside one of the barracks) to a sophisticated camera for the forgers (obtained by one of the guards in exchange for the return of his purloined identity papers). Thorp's cohort had its own "scrounger" as well; "sure, just like in the movie." However, Thorp was quick to add that the "greatness" of the Great Escape was not in these sorts of preparations and procurements, but in the escapees' diversion of German time and energy away from the war.

Many prisoners applied the same ingenuity that went into escape attempts to the challenge of modifying their circumstances to their own liking, he noted. Making do and obtaining forbidden items was their forte. Thorp was familiar with the prisoners' practice of making compass housings out of old Victrola records, cutting them into pieces which they softened by heating and then pressed into molds carved from bars of soap. He also reported that a radio had somehow been obtained—probably through bribery—enabling the Allies to listen to the BBC. German radio was played over the camp loudspeaker; consequently they could hear both the German and BBC versions of the war. He claimed that both sides greatly exaggerated their victories and discreetly minimized their losses. According to German radio reports, the German army never retreated but rather "took up new positions." Thorp said that the prisoners of war would listen to the German and British reports and then apply a formula of dividing and adding to come up with an accurate picture of the war's progress.

In Stalag Luft III, the inmates were very fortunate to be reasonably well treated. The camp commandant in the movie salutes the senior British officer, Group Captain Ramsay (James Donald), and repeatedly uses "please and thank you" when conversing with the high-ranking British prisoners. Thorp emphasized that Stalag Luft III was a camp for Allied air force officers operated by German air force officers, resulting in a virtual fraternity of pilots. In addition to British and American airmen, Polish and Dutch pilots were also incarcerated there. The Luftwaffe seemed to consider the Allied airmen more as brother pilots than as enemy prisoners. Thorp stressed that until the Great Escape and the murder of the fifty recaptured prisoners, it seemed as if the Germans and their British prisoners were playing a "cat and mouse game." Over and over again, the Brits would escape, eventually be recaptured and returned to the camp, only to escape and start the entire procedure over again. He called the Brits "escape-minded." They had been captured early in the war when the Allied cause seemed very gloomy, and they did not have the same optimism as some of the recently imprisoned Americans who believed that the war would soon be successfully ended.

This idea that the German captors and Allied (especially British) captives were engaged in a gamelike relationship was reinforced by a story Thorp heard, recounting an actual incident that took place before he arrived in camp. Apparently, in one compound no showers were provided for the prisoners, and they were forced to make do with only limited washing facilities. After numerous complaints lodged by the high-ranking Brits went unheeded, they decided to take matters into their own hands. A couple of British officers who spoke fluent German dressed up in German guard uniforms that had been provided for them by the camp's "excellent tailors," marched several prisoners up to the compound gate and announced to the German guards that they were taking their prisoners to another compound for showers. The gates were flung open wide, and it wasn't until the shower bound men had gone some distance that the impostors were recognized and "escorted" back to the their proper area. Eventually, the British officers arranged to have a shower house built in their compound. The Third Reich was unwilling to pay for this convenience, so the Brits stood the expense themselves.

Similarly, in the movie, ingenious Allied airmen never shrink from confronting their German captors with their demands, or circumventing Teutonic rules and regulations. In the film, it is obvious that the ranking British officer considers himself at least the equal of the German commandant, and at the end of the film, the British officer *demands* to know exactly how many of the prisoners "shot while trying to escape" were merely wounded, rather than killed. When the commandant does not reply, the British officer demands in a bolder, louder, and more insistent voice. Thorp verified that the exact words used by the British officer in the film were the ones heard by the prisoners who witnessed this exchange between the British and German commanding officers.

While the Luftwaffe officers treated their prisoners well, some of the guards were less polite in their dealings with their charges. Thorp explained that the Germans on guard duty were generally soldiers not fit for fighting on the frontlines. Some had been wounded earlier in the war and were assigned to the less rigorous duty of prison guards. Most of these guards were "okay"; however, a few were rough on the prisoners, and only too happy to be given any excuse to strike or shoot an insubordinate man.

Thorp related a story about a group of Allied airmen who were mistakenly dispatched to a concentration camp. He explained that when a prisoner of war escaped, he always took with him some part of his own uniform—a button, a medal—anything that would identify him as a prisoner-of-war escapee, so he would not be mistaken for a spy. Some escapees, however, were still labeled spies and sent to one of the camps. When the Luftwaffe discovered this error, they rescued the airmen and brought them to Stalag Luft III. Thorp said the heads of the men were shaved, and they were starving—"wild eyed, like animals." His response to recent talk of compensating concentration camp inmates was to maintain that "no amount of money could compensate for the pain and suffering of those in concentration camps." According to Thorp's recollections, life in Stalag Luft III was, for the most part, tolerable.

The one necessity there was never enough of was food. The rations they were allotted by the Germans were meager and less than appetizing, and the prisoners were hungry nearly all of the time. When the Allied commanding officer complained to the camp commandant, he was informed that the prisoners were being allocated the same food in the same amounts as the German soldiers. The Red Cross packages containing the food the prisoners craved arrived only sporadically, and so they were precious. Thorp disgusted his British friends by chewing the same stick of Red Cross gum for several days. He would stick it to his bedpost every night—a habit similar to that of Colin Blythe (Donald Pleasance), the chief forger in the film, who is shown reusing the same tea bag, day after day.

Thorp didn't smoke, and since cigarettes were included in the Red Cross packages, he was able to use his supply to trade for other items in the barter economy that sprang up within the camp. According to Thorp, candy bars were the most valuable items in Red Cross packages. Apparently one could "buy" anything with a candy bar. One prisoner from Georgia paid one hundred dollars for a single candy bar: he wrote his check out on a blank piece of paper, and it was reported that after the war, checks such as these were indeed honored by his bank.

Some details of everyday life, however, did differ from those depicted in the movies. Thorp said that contrary to some people's preconceptions, women were not much thought of or talked about in the camp. He saw no Betty Grable pinups in Stalag Luft III, unlike those depicted in film. Thorp claimed that the only time women were given much thought at all was after a Christmas "bash." The men had saved delicacies from the Red Cross and edible gifts from home. After the party, Thorp said that for the first and only time while he was imprisoned, the men talked of women, and some of the Brits sang a raunchy song. Food was what everyone desired, and Thorp often dreamed of food, but never of Betty Grable.

Other activities were also focused on taking prisoners' minds off their confinement, including dramatic productions. He recalled that the British prisoners put on some "high-class shows." Every two weeks a new production would open, and tickets were not always easy to obtain. This type of entertainment was very popular with the men in the camp. Elaborate scenery was painted, and props were somehow obtained or transformed from other items available in camp. Thorp explained that the costumes were rented—from a theatrical costume agency in Berlin! He was slightly disappointed because he had tried out for an all-American production but didn't get the part. Likewise, in *The Great Escape,* no idle men are seen; everyone is involved in some type of activity, although the activity might not be exactly what their guards think it is.

The prisoners of war who were incarcerated together in the Stalag still often get together, and what they celebrate is not V-E Day or V-J Day but rather their "anniversary—April 29, 1945, when tanks from Patton's army knocked down the gates" that had kept the Allied prisoners confined until the day they were liberated. Thorp recalled: "The greatest sight I ever saw was when the swastika went down and the Stars and Stripes went up. It was the happiest day of my life!" Thorp remembered attending several reunions for airmen who were in Stalag Luft III. These reunions are not limited to just the imprisoned Allies. He said that the German guards attended as well as the German women who as young girls read and censored the mail of the Allied prisoners. Even more surprising is that after the war, the ranking British and American officers who had been interned in Stalag Luft III during the Luftwaffe commandant's tenure returned to Germany and testified on his behalf at a war crimes trial—attesting to the respectful and humane treatment they received while they were his prisoners.

With Lieutenant Thorp to bear witness, it is no idle boast on the part of the filmmaker that "every detail of the escape is the way it really happened." Although Thorp's involvement in the war ended fifty-two years ago, he is still a pilot today, as are his two sons. He claims that even now when flying his plane, he can look out "and see B-17s in formation and all of the black puffs from flak." He remembers Stalag Luft III and the nine months he spent confined on the same German soil that had quartered the bold men who dared the Great Escape.

7

CODE TALKERS, *WINDTALKERS*, AND *TRUE WHISPERS*

Thomas Begay is one of four surviving World War II Navajo code talkers who fought at Saipan. He served not only in that war, but also in Korea. As did all of the World War II code talkers, Begay had remained silent (as per military orders) about his war contributions until the story of the Navajo Marine code talkers was finally declassified in 1969. Until that time, not even his wife knew of the code or that her husband had been selected to be a code talker.

On December 7, 1941, Begay was attending a U.S. boarding school for Native Americans in Arizona. He was playing football when news of Pearl Harbor and America's entrance into the war reached him—one of his friends came running onto the field, announcing that the Japanese had attacked. However, it wasn't until almost two years later, in August 1943, that Begay, now living on a Navajo reservation, was recruited to serve in the war. When asked how old he was when he enlisted in the Marines, Begay's answer was simply, "old enough."[1] He did acknowledge, however, that he was so young that his mother had to sign a consent form before he could be conscripted. His mother couldn't write but indicated her approval of his joining by "making a thumb mark." During World War II, the Marines were known to enlist very young men and Begay, apparently, was one of them. (He admits that he was only a ninth grader but decided that his age was "flexible" when he enlisted.)

According to Begay, the Marine recruiter appealed to the young would-be warriors on the reservation by explaining that the Japanese were trying to take the land away—all of the land—including the land that they called home. That was enough to make this young Navajo fighting mad. Originally he wanted to be an aerial gunner; however, Begay was dispatched to code talking school in California. Not all Navajo recruits were well suited to be code talkers. Begay recalled that the ability to learn and use the code—to learn the word substitutions on which it depended, and translate messages into and out of the code quickly and accurately—varied across individuals much like any other skill. He noted that of the approximately one hundred prospective code talkers in his class, nearly one-third dropped out of the program: "They couldn't comprehend it." But Begay did. He demonstrated the basic principle behind this code: the substitution of everyday Navajo words for military terms that had no actual equivalent in the Navajo language. Thus the Navajo word for "potato" referred to a hand grenade, and the Navajo for "egg" meant bomb. He went on, the code indelibly recorded in his memory.

The Marine Corps had, in the years between the world wars, made assaults on enemy-held beaches one of their combat specialties. They developed specialized weapons, equipment, and tactics for such operations, and practiced the necessary skills on peacetime beaches. Those skills made the Marines vital players in the Pacific War, thanks to the U.S. strategy of "island hopping," which called for rolling back Japanese territorial advances one island group at a time. As American forces advanced westward from Hawaii, the Marines led the way in assault after assault, seizing and holding a beachhead onto which the Army could disembark. The path to a defeated Japan wound through dozens of scattered archipelagoes and isolated islands, and Begay was present at many of the battles: the Marshall Islands, Guam, and Saipan.

All of these assaults were made far more dangerous by the Japanese army's defensive preparations on the islands. "There were snipers all around," Begay remembered. Life was dangerous for code-talking radio men, partly because doing their job required that they be in the thick of frontline combat, and partly because the bulky field radios of the era were heavy and cumbersome, making it difficult to move or seek cover. Radio operators were, like officers, favorite targets for enemy fire since killing them would sow confusion as well as diminish the ranks of the American invaders. During battle, Begay recounted how he had to change positions constantly before the Japanese were able to pinpoint his location.

Begay particularly remembered the invasion of Iwo Jima on February 19, 1945. The island, with its vital airfield and craggy volcanic interior dominated by Mount Suribachi, was an especially difficult objective. The Japanese had, by January 1945, nearly two years to observe Marine assaults on other islands and fortify the beaches and interior of Iwo Jima. The island had to be taken, however, in order to gain control of its airfield. By 6:00 a.m. Begay had tested his radio and his weapon, and was ready to go. The landing was scheduled to take place at 9:00 a.m. Before hitting the beach, the Marines were fed steak and eggs for breakfast (it was later realized that this heavy meal did, literally, weigh down Marines and make their landing more difficult). During the landing Begay "felt numb." He recalled being the target of a sniper's bullet, and at the time wasn't certain if he had been wounded or not. Fortunately, the sniper missed his mark. While things weren't too bad during the Marine landing, once all of them were on the beach, the Japanese "opened up . . . everything came down." Enemy fire rained on the newly landed troops and the Marines lost five code talkers that day—either killed or wounded during the initial barrage. The battle raged on. Begay was on the island and in the thick of battle for thirty-eight straight days; in the first forty-eight hour period, the code talkers sent and received eight hundred messages without an error.

Begay claimed that seeing the American flag raised on Iwo Jima's Mount Suribachi a moment captured in the iconic Joe Rosenthal photograph that became the inspiration for the Marine Corps Memorial— was one of the grandest sights of his life. As often is the case with combat veterans, he did not offer many details of his combat experiences and preferred not to dwell on the horrors of war. However, he was very proud to repeat the words of his commanding officer, Major Howard M. Cooper: "Were it not for the Navajos, the Marines never would have taken Iwo Jima." He proudly quoted another senior officer who stated that because of the service of the Navajo, "many lives were saved."

Although Begay did not reference his own military record, the program for a pow wow at which he was honored stated: "Begay was awarded six battle stars during his Marine/Army career, which stretched from Iwo Jima to Korea. He was also awarded the Presidential Unit Citation with three Bronze Stars and the Meritorious Unit Citation with the Korean Service medal with five Bronze service stars." The event was the Veterans Friendship Pow Wow—A Gathering for Healing, Restoration and Peace. The program stated: "Honoring warriors is a strong tradition among Native American people" and instructed: "Since it is the tradition of Native Americans to honor veterans and their families, studies have shown that veterans of Native American tribes have the lowest rate of post war [sic] trauma. These ceremonies help the warrior to heal." Against the backdrop of a cloudless blue sky, there was singing, drumming, and dancing. Begay spoke to the crowd of his code talking experiences, explaining and demonstrating the code. As the Native dancers moved past him, they dropped money at his feet, to honor him and express gratitude for his service.

When the subject of John Woo's film, *Windtalkers*, came up, Begay gestured a very definite thumbs down: "That was Hollywood stuff." The former code talker believed that director Woo just "wanted to make money." Begay had applied to be a consultant on the film, but "they hired some guy from Los Angeles who was not a code talker—in fact, he couldn't speak Navajo and wasn't familiar with the culture." Begay was disappointed that he did not get this consulting job since he was obviously well qualified. It was, he felt, "all politics."

The former code talker seemed insulted by the lack of authenticity in the film's portrayal of the code talkers. He referenced one code talker (actor) in the film who was "fat," in contrast to all of the other Marines, who were in "tip-top shape." In fact, this onetime code talker had nothing good to say about the film's historical accuracy. Begay seemed to believe that history was not even consulted when producing the film—that concern for producing a profitable film rendered history, and even reality, irrelevant.

"Inspired by true events,"[2] the story line of *Windtalkers* is that U.S. Marine Joe Enders (Nicholas Cage) is assigned to act as bodyguard to Navajo code talker Ben Yahzee (Adam Beach). Enders has been told by his superiors to "protect the code at all costs," with an emphasis on "all" that leaves no doubt he is to kill Yahzee rather than allow him to be taken alive by the Japanese. When the two are sent ashore during the invasion of Saipan in June 1944 and capture seems imminent, Enders—already psychologically scarred by memories of losing men under his command in combat—must confront the possibility that he will have to execute the man he has sworn to protect and grown to like and respect. Eventually, on the verge of being overrun by the Japanese and seemingly out of options, he resolves his dilemma by calling for Marine artillery to lay down a

Figure 7.1. The story of the Navajo code talkers was declassified in 1969, and inspired the story of John Woo's *Windtalkers*.

barrage suicidally close to their position. According to Begay, this body-guard scenario was pure fiction: "No; that's a bunch of lies." However, fears about the code being cracked were real. He cites a Marine from New Mexico, fighting in the Philippines, who was taken prisoner by the Japanese and tortured to give up the code, though he never did. According to Begay, the man may have been a Navajo, but "he was not a code talker." Chester Nez, who served as a code talker in the Pacific, said that he "was never aware of having bodyguard" and had never heard of a code talker being killed to protect the code: "I don't think it ever happened."[3] Nez related that he and his fellow code talkers don't remember being paired with another marine.

Captain Matt Morgan from the Marine Corps' Public Affairs Office confirms the veterans' memories: "Aside from the premise, which is em-bellishment, the film's very accurate." And the premise? "It's a dramatic concept really . . . an interesting notion."[4] Richard Schickel's *Time* maga-zine review of Woo's film explains that the mission *to protect the code at all costs* "exists as a largely unexamined premise, while the picture pur-sues a more routinely uplifting theme of male bonding across fairly stan-dard barriers of ignorance and prejudice."[5] Like Begay, Nez refers to parts of the film as "pure Hollywood." He recalls a scene in the film depicting Navajo ceremonies. "In a combat area you don't do something like that, you know. It's Hollywood."

A *Christian Science Monitor* reviewer takes the same view, pointing out that "Not particularly interested in letting the facts get in the way of a good story, the filmmakers have changed a few elements, calling the film 'inspired by true events.'"[6] Similarly, the BBC's Neil Smith observes: "This being a John Woo movie, such ethical considerations take second place to epic scenes of explosive destruction that make Pearl Harbor look like a skirmish in a bath tub,"[7] but a CNN.com reviewer remains unimpressed: "no amount of burning, blasting, stabbing and shooting can hide a bad script,"[8] observing that the film relies on "a wishy-washy storyline that feints toward importance while settling for blood-and-guts and a string of 'war is hell' clichés. Some of these scenes would make John Wayne blush."[9]

Historian Lawrence Suid agrees: "Despite its lofty goals, the motion picture *Windtalkers* . . . does little to enhance the image of the U.S. Marine Corps or give the Navajo code talkers their due."[10] He refers to a statement by Matt Morgan, Marine public affairs officer: "This was never a standing order and it is certainly an illegal one. Marines operating in this manner smacks of some kind of Bushido ideal implying the Corps works like a Shogunate. Not so, of course."[11] Interestingly enough, however, according to Morgan, the producer had talked to Navajo code talkers who believed that such an order existed during World War II and had created the script on the basis of that belief: "If the Marines had insisted on an accurate portrayal of the code talkers' relationships with their fellow Marines, then the producer would have no film."[12] Faced with this "at all costs" issue, Morgan proposed a "simple fix" for the film's troubling subject matter: "Ender's orders should be simple, giving him the intent of his assignment, and leaving the specifics up to his 'warrior instincts.'" Morgan explained that "Any good Marine 'worth his salt' would understand. . . . Problem solved. Enders is left to deal with the ambiguity on his own . . . and the question of murdering the code talkers is a moral dilemma no different than a combat leader's decision to call in final protective fire." Even if Enders's orders were not as blunt as "kill the code talker," *Windtalkers* "left little doubt about what the white bodyguards were supposed to do if their Indian charges were facing imminent capture. . . . In the end, therefore, the Marines helped to perpetuate a myth rather than tell the truth, that code talkers simply did their jobs, with the only threat to their lives coming from the enemy."[13] Suid observes that "worse than the myth-making and the denial of history, *Windtalkers* fails in its stated purpose of giving the code talkers their due."[14] Undeniably, the film revolves around white Marine Ender's haunting demons; the code talkers are simply a background presence.

A *Grand Rapids Press* reviewer, who had volunteered in a private school that serves the 25,000-square-mile Navajo nation in the Four Corners area, notes that Ben Yahzee does not even behave like a typical Navajo young man: "He displays a certain air of confidence not found in most Navajo. He's a joiner, is affable and enjoys engaging in conversations while using his sense of humor. These traits stand in contrast to his Navajo brothers and sisters."[15] However the reviewer, who had lived and worked with the Navajo and had also interviewed a code talker, suggested that, to many white Marines, the Navajo could be mistaken for Japanese and be in danger from their own comrades-in-arms. "This put the Navajos in extreme peril and caused some to be captured by their fellow Marines. Since the Navajo were dressed in American uniforms, they were considered spies and could be shot . . . the result was that, after several close calls, each Navajo code talker was assigned a *bilagaana* [white] Marine bodyguard for protection against confused American soldiers."[16] Code talker Chester Nez adds credence to this assertion: "I didn't have anyone following me, nor did I see guys who did. . . . But once, I had a G.I. who thought I was Japanese and"—Nez makes a gun with this right hand and presses it to his forehead—"he put a .45 right there. It seemed as big as a cannon. . . . That was not fun."[17]

Nez points out that, ironically, from the beginning of the twentieth century, U.S. government policy aimed at Navajo assimilation banned the Navajo language. "All of those years telling you not to speak Navajo; and then to turn around and ask us for help with that same language . . . it still kind of bothers me."[18] Thomas Begay and the film's reviewers agree:

> The biggest clichés are the Navajos . . . *Windtalkers* takes a wide-eyed Noble Savage New Age-y view of all things Navajo. They are a deeply spiritual people. They play flute music, chant prayers and blow smoke. They are One with Nature. Not unlike the portraits of Jews and African Americans in the social problem films of the post-war era, the earnest efforts to celebrate a minority group drip with condescension. The Indians here are, well, wooden.[19]

Consensus was that *"Windtalkers* falls victim to Hollywood romanticism—too many bigoted soldiers making stereotypical jokes about "Injuns" until they eventually come to respect the loyal, spiritual, brave Navajo, who started out code talkers but ended up Marines."[20]

Even before its release, *Windtalkers* was unpopular with real-life code talkers. Navajo Code Talkers Association president Samuel Billisone said, "I'd like to see them use Native American actors, but first to get authorization from the Navajo Code Talkers Association. . . . We're a nonprofit organization. These people make millions of dollars and we don't get anything, and they make a lot of mistakes."[21] Begay concurred: "I didn't get a rusty penny." Of those Navajo code talkers who spoke about the film, the verdict seemed to be unanimous: the film falls far short of achieving its claimed goal: to honor these Navajo warriors' unique contributions to the Pacific War. Rather, the film is simply another Hollywood war film, with the white hero front and center.

There is, however, another film about the code talkers—a very different kind of film. *True Whispers: The Story of the Navajo Code Talkers* is a documentary in which the code talkers actually participated. The film places the code talkers and their story front and center. It offers contextual background for the use of Navajo code talkers, explaining that during the war, the Japanese were highly adept at breaking Allied code, and the U.S. military, being badly beaten in the Pacific, needed an unbreakable code. Philip Johnston, the son of a missionary on the Navajo reservation, is credited with initiating the idea of using the Navajo language as the basis for a new code. Johnston grew up on the reservation, playing with Navajo children, and learned to speak his friends' language. At nine years old, the young Johnston traveled to Washington, DC, with his father and local Navajo leaders to petition the president for more land, serving as translator between the Navajo and then president Theodore Roosevelt. Johnston left the reservation to attend college in California, where he remained, but he maintained his ties with the Navajo community. After the Japanese attack on Pearl Harbor, Johnston submitted a proposal to the Marines to utilize the Navajo language to transmit military orders. After a demonstration using local Navajo speakers, a coding system was developed; in 1942 the Navajo Code Talker program was initiated, and the first all-Navajo platoon was graduated from San Diego's Marine Corps Recruit Depot.

True Whispers relates the story of those Navajo who, like Begay, answered their country's call to duty during World War II. The Navajo language was needed—Navajo were needed—precisely because there were few Navajo speakers, and virtually no nonnative speakers. The obscurity of the language and the difficulty of learning it, made the code so secure in the first place. The irony of this was enormous: not only did the code rely on a Navajo culture that the United States had spent years endeavoring to stamp out of existence, but the code talkers were often recruited from the same Indian boarding schools that were the principal tool for eradicating the native language. Many of those who served their country by speaking Navajo had spent their youth in schools that forbade them from speaking it under threat of painful physical punishment. While telling the story of the Navajo code talkers, the film does much to relate the culture of these first Americans and the U.S. policy of cultural annihilation.

True Whispers opens with current-day images of Navajo country. The audience sees a desert landscape, ancestral home of the Navajo for thousands of years. Throughout the film, the Navajo code talkers speak of their connection to this land—Mother Earth—and the "sacred mountains" rising from it. But unlike the cliché-riddled "close to nature" stereotypes found in *Windtalkers*, these descriptions originate from the Navajo themselves, and are framed within the context of their own worldview.

Code talker Begay opens the film describing how, as a boy, he was awakened before dawn to herd sheep. He was living the traditional Navajo life, and "life was good." But then he describes the day U.S. officials came and took him from his family and placed him in one of the notorious culture-killing boarding schools. Over stills of these now-infamous schools, voices of other code talkers divulge the horrors and sadness they experienced in similar schools, as what one man described as "prisoners." In an especially effective scene, a posed group picture of these young students dissolved into a posed picture of the Marine Corps 382nd Platoon of code talkers—wearing the uniforms of the country that had been attempting to eradicate Navajo culture for the previous seventy-five years.

The film unfolds, mixing nineteenth- and twentieth-century photos, World War II–era stills, archival footage, and present-day interviews with remaining code talkers. The now senior Navajo relate how they were sent to basic training, which was "not too bad" because, as one of their commanding officers observed, the Navajo were already in great physical condition when they arrived at camp—much better condition than most new marines. After basic training, the young Navajo were sent to Camp Pendleton, where their top-secret work began. Here these young Native Americans were required to construct an unbreakable code. As we view photos of these young Marines working to devise their impregnable code based on their unique language, the voices of the now elderly code talkers describe the code that was conceived. Today, this once top-secret, classified code can easily be found on the Internet.

In interviews, code talkers relate how their code worked: a message was given to them in written English, which they translated into the unique Navajo code, and then safely transmitted in standard Morse code. By the end of his training, a code talker could receive, translate, and send a three-line message in a mere twenty seconds. The code talkers explained that they did not just memorize one code; they had to commit to memory three separate codes. After training, these young soon-to-be warriors returned home where they took part in traditional Protection Way ceremonies designed to keep them safe in battle. *True Whispers* reenacts one of these ceremonies as the voices of the code talkers relate how the elders in their communities performed songs, prayers, and rituals for the young man's safe return.

The film stresses the importance of the code in the Pacific victories: Guadalcanal, Bougainville, Saipan, and Tarawa among others, but most especially Iwo Jima. Through documentary footage, the audience witnesses the horrors of this most bloody battle, as the voices of code talkers relate their own experiences during combat. During this hellish battle, many code talkers volunteered to replace fallen Marines on the frontlines. As a Marine Signal Officer observes, "Were it not for the Navajos, the United States could have never taken Iwo Jima."

After the war, the Navajo returned home under strict orders not to speak a word about the code or their war contributions. They received no high rank, no medals, and, for the most part, no veteran's benefits. Like many returning veterans, one code talker spoke of the war's aftermath. He experienced nightmares in which he was haunted by the spirit of an enemy soldier he killed. Eventually, he consulted a medicine man who performed the Enemy Way ceremony, designed to lay the ghost of the dead man to rest. The elderly code talker reported that after the ceremony, his nightmares ended; as the medicine man stated, the code talker had been "restored."

In 1968 the code was declassified and code talkers could finally speak of their war, and on August 14, 1982, their contributions were made public. In 2001, the remaining code talkers received Congressional Gold and Silver Medals presented to them by President George W. Bush. This recognition was a long time coming. The film continues from the Washington, DC, ceremony to present-day images of the Navajo reservation, where Navajo families live on less than $12,000 a year and where Navajo still have to fight for water rights, land rights, and fishing and hunting rights.

As this reflective, thought-provoking film ends, we see age-faded warriors marching down the road, carrying their flags, and being cheered by young Navajo admirers. The Marine Corps anthem is heard in the background, sung in Navajo. On-screen, a code talker recalls the horrors of war, yet states: "If it happened again, I would do the whole thing again." Against a backdrop of the poverty and hardship of the reservation, another relates that he went to fight because a foreign country was trying to take Navajo "Mother Earth"; he also is "ready to go again." The code talkers continue to march, the bystanders cheer, and "The Star-Spangled Banner" is sung . . . in Navajo.

8

THE ROSIES: LUCY, GOLDIE, GINGER, AND MARGE

Millions of American men were involved with the fighting and winning of World War II; millions of American women were, too. There were 350,000 women who wore uniforms during the war, including the heroic members of the Army and Navy Nurse Corps who cared for wounded servicemen—often just behind the frontlines—along with members of the various services' women's auxiliary corps. Women took over administrative and clerical work, as well as technical jobs, and members of the Women's Air Service Pilots, a uniformed civilian organization, towed aerial gunnery targets, transported passengers and cargo, and delivered combat-ready aircraft—including high-performance single-engine fighters and heavy bombers—from factories to Army airfields.

Millions more women, without actually enlisting, did their part—a very large part—for the war effort. Members of the "Hidden Army," they stepped up to fill the civilian jobs left by men, and took on the new jobs created to serve the production needs of the war: everything from assembling delicate electronic components to welding the hulls of Liberty Ships and riveting tanks and aircraft. "Rosie the Riveter," the fictional heroine of a hit song and a recruiting poster declaring "We Can Do It!" represented them all. At the time, many believed that women could never successfully take the place of men in these jobs, but America's "Rosies" proved them wrong. A great many of them did so, moreover, while continuing to keep their houses, raise their children, and dealing with the myriad ways—coping with gasoline and food rationing, planting victory gardens, and saving household fats for use in munitions plants—that Americans were exhorted to "do their bit" for the war effort. Marge Mehlberg and Lucille Broderick were two of them.

On December 7, 1941, Marge Mehlberg was living in Sidney, Illinois, teaching first and second grades. Like millions of other Americans she received the news of the attack on Pearl Harbor from the radio. Her home was near an Army Air Forces base, and the military men always attended church in their civilian clothes. However, that Sunday, they all attended evening services in their uniforms.[1] Mehlberg was only twenty years old that December, and her life was to change drastically as the men in her community left for the military. The young schoolteacher learned to cut meat and, in the summer of 1942, took the place of the town's butcher, who had enlisted in the military. The following summer, however, she took off her butcher's apron and donned the coveralls and headscarf of a factory worker. She left her small hometown for Joliet, Illinois, and the Elwood Ordnance Factory, going to work on a shop floor that was, by then, staffed primarily by women. Her assignment, weighing explosives for bombs, was both exacting and dangerous, and the plant—for obvious reasons—operated under strict security. She and her fellow workers wore identification badges and were checked in and out of the plant individually at the end of their shift. Their lunch boxes were also inspected daily, to ensure that nothing was smuggled in or out of the plant. She later commented that had she been older and more experienced, she would have never taken such a dangerous job.

A year later, in the summer of 1944, Mehlberg—like thousands of American women and their cinematic counterparts—headed west. The war had produced boom times in California, expanding military bases, shipyards, aircraft plants, and other factories, and all of them were desperate for workers. Boarding the Santa Fe Railroad's sleek *El Capitan* streamliner at the Joliet station, she headed for Los Angeles, where an employment agency put her to work for Northrop Aircraft. Workers were at a premium, and Mehlberg and her coworkers were provided housing and transportation to and from work. Although Mehlberg landed a desk job at Northrop, her housemates did work on the factory floor building the P-61 night fighter, nicknamed the "Black Widow." Equipped with a remotely operated gun turret and onboard radar set for tracking enemy aircraft in darkness or bad weather, the Black Widow was on the cutting edge of military aviation. It was the highest of high technology . . . and it was riveted, assembled, and wired by women who, before the war, had likely never seen the inside of an airplane, much less an airplane factory. Mehlberg recalled that while working for the aircraft company, all the women needed to abide by rules of conduct. She pulled out her *Code of Conduct Handbook* and pointed out the numbered rules—fifty-four of them. First and foremost among these, the women were never to mention the name Northop; her work for the defense company was all "very secretive." Each day, when she and her coworkers entered the Northop building, their badges were checked, and, according to their badge numbers, they were restricted from certain areas in the building.

Another woman who clocked in hours on the factory floor during the war was Lucille Broderick of Bloomington, Illinois. She was married and had a six-month-old daughter when, driving home from a family dinner, she heard newsboys shouting, announcing a special edition of the paper reporting Japan's attack on Pearl Harbor. Before too long, the couple and their daughter left their home in the central Illinois town of Bloomington and moved to the St. Louis area where her husband Jim found work in a munitions factory. He was over thirty, married with a child, and thus deferred from the draft. However, he returned home one night after work to tell Lucille that he had enlisted in the Navy. After boot camp at the Great Lakes and some additional training at Iowa State University, he left his wife and daughter and caught a train for the West Coast. In California he boarded the aircraft carrier *Corregidor* and sailed for the South Pacific, where he spent the duration of the war. [2]

Lucille Broderick was left to keep the home fires burning and to care for their little girl. She took a job at a local factory, Williams Oil-A-Matic, which had once produced furnaces but had been converted to support the war effort. One of her sisters and one of her sisters-in-law already worked at Williams when Broderick began there. The pay was better than any job she had held previously, and for the first time in her life, she was working alongside African American women. There was hardly a man in sight—the factory was now staffed almost entirely by women. However, the few men who were still on the floor were "not too happy to see the women there." For the first six months she was at "the plant," Broderick worked on a line assembling furnace motors; however, she was moved to another area and began doing "government work." Her pay was immediately increased from seventy-five cents an hour to ninety cents, thanks to Uncle Sam. A good wage, for a woman, though she still gets perturbed recalling that men doing the same job were paid more. Broderick noted that most of the women she worked with had husbands "in the war."

When women like Mehlberg and Broderick went to the movies to relax, they would have regularly encountered films about women's contributions to the war effort. Scores of government-funded documentary shorts exhorted audiences to plant gardens, recycle strategic materials, cheerfully comply with rationing programs, and buy war bonds, all in the name of Victory. Some, like *The Hidden Army* (produced by the U.S. Army Signal Corps), addressed women factory workers specifically, praising those already on the line for their contributions and shaming those who remained at home rather than attending to war work. The film opened with an image from the hoped-for future: Hitler, jailed and awaiting execution, lamenting in his memoirs that his greatest mistake was underestimating American women. Declaring that Germany sees American women as "playgirls—pampered and spoiled," who care only for "cosmetics and silk stockings," the narrator intones: "American women, aren't you going to prove our enemy wrong?" When the narrator questions women on the factory floor about why they took on war work, all of them responded with patriotic answers. The film ends with a picture of "The finest warrior—the greatest woman of them all": the Statue of Liberty.[3]

This appeal to national pride was, ironically, wrapped in extensive reassurances to its female target audience about the accommodations that had been made because it was "difficult to be a housekeeper and a patriot."[4] Stores now stay open late to adapt to the hours of the women on the line. Transportation and childcare are being provided for the factory workers. The women could pick up their ration coupons and renew their driver's license at the plant. Fulfilling one's responsibilities as a patriotic American was, the film implied, no barrier to fulfilling one's responsibilities as a conventional wife and mother. A shot of a woman weeping over a telegram announcing the death of a loved one with the dreaded words: "The government regrets to inform you . . ." hinted darkly at the cost of slacking. A woman's failure to do war work (and keep the men at the front supplied with what they needed) was, the film implied, a failure to protect her (or her neighbor's) husband or son.

Hollywood feature films, too, illustrated how American women at home could, and did, do their "bit" in the Allies' eventual triumph. Hollywood portrayed valiant women in uniformed service (*So Proudly We Hail*, 1943) and holding home and family together in the face of Nazi attacks (*Mrs. Miniver*, 1942), but they also showed "ordinary" women like those in the audience making contributions on the home front. The women in these films took jobs, handled the inconvenience of rationing, dealt with housing shortages, and cared for children, all while living in loneliness and in fear of "the Telegram."

Tender Comrade, a 1943 film directed by Edward Dmytryk, is a typical "women's picture" of the era, revolving around the marital and interpersonal dramas of four women thrown together by the war. It is also, however, a full-throttle piece of propaganda designed to instruct and inspire women on the home front under the guise of entertainment. Jo Jones (Ginger Rogers) is an American everywoman, working at the Douglas Aircraft plant and caring for her infant son while her husband Chris (Robert Ryan) fights to preserve democracy and make the world a better place. Jo proposes to three fellow workers that they pool their salaries and rent a house together, equally dividing whatever money is left over after their expenses have been paid. They agree, and set about communal housekeeping, working together for the good of all. While Broderick could not recall seeing *Tender Comrade*, she was part of a very large family, and was sharing housing with sisters and sisters-in-law. She also remembered the women at home often pooling their food rations together in order to enjoy tastier meals rather than their usual fare of "hot dogs, bologna, and sausages."

The four women in *Tender Comrade* represent a wide range of homefront experiences. Jo, happily married, misses her husband desperately, and frets (via flashback) over past moments where she troubled him unnecessarily. Barbara, serially unfaithful to her own absent husband Pete, goes on dates and frequents nightclubs, while newlywed Doris laments the fact that her husband's rapid deployment overseas—literally on their wedding day—left their marriage unconsummated. Helen, older, has both a husband and an adult son in uniform. Melodrama, romantic and otherwise, abounds. Barbara expresses her skepticism about the need for rationing, and displays her contempt for Pete by inviting her "dates" to pick her up at home, and is chastised for both by her housemates. Conversely, when Doris's husband is granted unexpected leave, her housemates rally around her, cooking a special supper for the couple as a prelude to their long-delayed "wedding night." Even as it goes through

ALAMEDA FREE LIBRARY

the motions expected of a women's picture, however, *Tender Comrades* never passes up an opportunity to deliver its wartime message.

Critic Manny Farber, in an acerbic review of the film published in *The New Republic* in 1944, says of the four women: "Theirs is the ideal wartime behavior for wives: knitting, gushing over their letters and pictures and persecuting one of their members who now and then threatens to go a night club and is somewhat unenthusiastic about rationing."[5] Jo and her roommates have "moral little chit-chats on devoting one's efforts on the war and keeping away from the fellows,"[6] and Jo in particular never seems to tire of reinforcing the egalitarian nature of their household: "[We'll] run it like a democracy . . . let's take a vote."[7] She also proclaims that the women "share and share alike," which, during the war, was a laudable sentiment. It was also one that, during the postwar Red Scare, would cause director Dmytryk and screenwriter Dalton Trumbo a considerable amount of trouble with the House Un-American Activities Committee.

Early in the film, the women hire a German housekeeper named Manya—a refugee who fled her native country because its rulers "murdered democracy," and whose husband (lest there be any lingering doubt) is fighting in the American Army. Manya, as an outsider, gives the women (mostly Jo) an audience to which they can "preach democracy,"[8] but she also serves as a judge of whether the American women are living up to their country's ideals. When a friendly butcher gives the household an extra pound of bacon to which their ration books do not entitle them, Manya denounces their eager acceptance of it as sinful and undemocratic "hoarding."

Praising democracy and educating this newcomer to democracy's principles and ideals is just what the OWI ordered. Even when her husband is reported dead, Jo submerges her sense of loss in a greater message about global democracy and freedom. She lectures her infant son, and the audience: "He went out and died so that you would have a break when you grow up. Don't ever forget that, little guy."[9]

The film's ideological stance is thus clear and consistent: solidarity, frugality, and vigilance are the watchwords of the day, and losses are to be borne stoically. As a critic for the *New Yorker* notes: "It is pointed out that rationing is a necessity and scarcely a hardship when you consider its purpose . . . and that when a father dies in this war, it is for something his children must continue to protect."[10] There is no exceptional bravery here: "The people in this picture are average people, who think, for the most part, as Americans should be thinking, and when one of them gets a little out of line, he or she is told off promptly and undergoes a quick, satisfactory reformation."[11] Having just learned that she has lost her husband, and must raise her child alone, Jo vows that she'll "take it on the chin like a good guy, like a soldier's wife should."

Since You Went Away (1944), described by one wartime reviewer as "the definitive American home-front movie,"[12] offers a similar mixture of "women's picture" melodrama and politics. Like *Tender Comrade*, it is centered on a tightly knit household of women—a "typical" upper-middle-class American family in an unnamed American town—whose members feel the touch of the war through its effects on the men they love. Like the women in *Tender Comrade*, albeit more subtly, some model "proper" and "expected" home-front behavior from the outset, while others must be educated, over the course of the film, until they do.

Anne Hilton (Claudette Colbert) is initially resentful of her husband Tim's determination to enlist. The (temporary) loss of the lucrative salary he earns as an advertising executive forces her to let go the family's beloved African American housekeeper, Fidelia (Hattie McDaniel), and take in a crusty retired Army officer, Colonel William Smollett, as a boarder. Lucille Broderick, like Anne, received a small government allotment—eighty dollars a month—while her husband was in uniform, but had trouble making do. Broderick came to depend on her salary, but when her factory offered extra weekend shifts she was, like countless other working women, torn between needing the overtime pay and not wanting to impose on family members who cared for her daughter while she worked. Although she would have liked the extra pay, she generally turned down weekend work.

Broderick remembered seeing *Since You Went Away*, and she could certainly relate to the film. Although housing and food rations were shared, one thing she said that no one (at least no one she knew) shared was cigarettes. She recalled how, at noon, "Some girls would go out to scout around to see if any stores or bars had cigarettes to sell." These women would report back, and if they had discovered some for sale, after getting off work, most of the people in the plant would make a beeline to the designated retailer.

In the film, Anne feels few economic pressures. Basic wartime economies, and the income she receives from Colonel Smollett is enough for her to maintain a comfortable upper-middle-class lifestyle. When she decides, late in the film, to take a job as a welder at a shipyard, the driving force is patriotism rather than economic need. *New York Times* film reviewer Bosley Crowther criticized the film at the time of its release for portraying an "average" family struggling with wartime finances while "their home is an absolute vision of well-decorated luxury."[13] Mehlberg and Broderick, however, both approved of the family's well-furnished and attractive home. As the latter observed, "That's the way the houses always looked in the movies." Crowther notes, however, that even in the midst of such inappropriately conspicuous consumption, the film "slipped in a scalding reflection here and there on people who trade on the black markets, hoard and do other hateful things."[14]

Anne's friend Emily Hawkins—a self-centered divorcée—is the main target of such criticism, but for most of the film Anne herself must be prodded by others to do her patriotic duty. Her decision to take on war work, for example, is kindled by her elder daughter Jane's desire to defer college and work as a nurse's aide, and by a chance encounter with a woman whose own daughter was posted as missing-in-action after the fall of the Philippines. Once she *does* don coveralls and pick up a welding torch, her decision is immediately reinforced by another chance encounter. An immigrant woman working alongside her describes the thrill she felt upon first reading the welcoming inscription on the Statue of Liberty, and declares Anne to be a living embodiment of the same spirit.

The sacrifices being demanded of those in uniform is, similarly, something that Anne must come to appreciate over the course of the film. Eager to repay a friendly shopkeeper for his kindness, she pledges Tim's help in securing a postwar job for the man's son, a trainee Army pilot, but the young aviator is killed in a crash only days later. Her daughter Jane (Jennifer Jones) falls in love with Colonel Smollett's grandson Bill, and by the time he receives orders to ship out, the two are planning to marry after the war. Their tearful good-bye at the railway station, however, proves to be their last meeting. A few months later, a telegram arrives for the Colonel, and Anne must tell her daughter that Bill has died in action. Anne has already received a telegram of her own—Tim is missing, and believed dead—but is spared her daughter's heartbreak. On Christmas Eve, as the family tearfully opens the presents Tim left behind before he was posted overseas, the phone rings. Tim is alive, and coming home.

Written, produced, and partly directed by Hollywood veteran David O. Selznick, *Since You Went Away* was immensely popular with audiences, earning $4,950,000 in North America during its theatrical release [15] and several Academy Award nominations. Selznick and his collaborators, like the makers of *Tender Comrade*, knew exactly who their audiences were, and carefully constructed their films to motivate as well as entertain them. One film ends with its heroine making a brave speech to her now-fatherless child, and the other with a joyous family celebrating the imminent return of an absent father, but both modeled the same idealized wartime behavior for American women: do your patriotic duty in support of the war effort, and bear whatever sacrifices the war imposes on you, without bitterness or questioning.

The war years were long since over, faded into hazy memories, when in 1984—four decades after *Tender Comrade* and *Since You Went Away*—another World War II home-front film was released to theaters. Jonathan Demme's *Swing Shift* looks back at the home front with forty years' worth of perspective, and does so with less emphasis on patriotism and sacrifice. War in *Swing Shift* is not all honor and glory. California housewife Kay Walsh (Goldie Hawn) takes a job in an aircraft plant to help fill her free time and do her patriotic duty after her husband Bob (Ed Harris) enlists in the Navy following Pearl Harbor. She has neither skills nor experience, but she learns fast, becoming a highly capable worker. She also strikes up friendships with her neighbor and fellow worker Hazel (Christine Lahti)—a part-time singer, whose boyfriend owns a nightclub—and her "leadman" (foreman), Mike "Lucky" Lockhart (Kurt Russell). Lucky, an easygoing trumpet player barred from military service by a heart condition, sets his romantic sights on Kay and—after months of overtures—she succumbs to his considerable charm. Their affair is cut short, however, when Bob returns home on leave. "Blame it on the war," he tells her, "that's everybody's excuse." [16] Later, when Bob leaves to return to his ship, he leaves her a note: "Everything changes. I'm different. You're different. The whole world is different." Referring to the war, he concludes: "It's [the war] sure taken its toll on all of us." [17]

Swing Shift received both praise and criticism for its attempt to actually duplicate 1940s home-front films. It was successful in creating an authentic look and feel—the clothes, the hairstyles, the homes, the music—Mehlberg agreed that the film got the look right—right down to the slacks that she and her friends wore. She added that Kay's (Hawn's)

Figure 8.1.   Kay (Goldie Hawn) and Hazel (Christine Lahti) do their bit to support the war in *Swing Shift*.

beautifully coiffed blond locks would have been the envy of the factory floor. Unlike Kay and Hazel, however, Mehlberg and her friends did not have wild social lives. The war hardly intrudes on all of the fun that Kay, Lucky, and Hazel are having. They go to dances, nightclubs, spend days at the beach, and drive to Mexico. Rationing is not in evidence, and there seems to be plenty of food, liquor, and cigarettes. The only hint of inconvenience is seen when Kay offers sugar to Hazel to sweeten the bitter tea they are drinking at that point in their relationship. Hazel raises an eyebrow: "You got sugar?"[18] News of the war barely registers on *Swing Shift*'s cinematic home front. Except when a voice comes over the factory's loud speaker, announcing Allied setbacks and urging the factory employees to work even harder, the global struggle to defeat Germany and Japan is a vague, distant presence.

Mehlberg remembers a very different kind of life: "pushing hard getting Black Widows completed," and putting in six- and seven-day workweeks that left little time or energy for dancing and flirting. Mehlberg was already engaged to her college boyfriend, who was serving in the Army Medical Corps. He was stationed in Hawaii where they were receiving casualties from all over the Pacific. Like Anne Hilton in *Since You Went Away* and Jo Jones in *Tender Comrade*, Mehlberg wrote, and wrote, and wrote to her fiancé in the Pacific and her brother in Europe. Broderick did the same, and confessed that there was still a box in her basement that contained a huge number of letters her husband had written to her, along with the ones that she had written to him, which he brought home after the war. The women of Mehlberg and Broderick's home front were glued to the radio for war news. Mehlberg remembers hearing Edward R. Murrow reporting from London, eagerly awaiting theatrical newsreels with scenes from the front, and gathering around the radio with friends and family to listen to President Roosevelt whenever he was on the air.

The film's most significant contribution, in fact, is to the conversation on the evolving role of women in relation to the war, paid employment, society, and each other. *New York* magazine's David Denby notes: "Kay is that familiar figure of feminist morality tales, a woman completely defined by her husband. . . . Yet when she sees a newsreel exhorting women to work in factories, she heads without a second's hesitation for her local aircraft plant and signs up."[19] Tellingly, Kay strikes up a friendship with Hazel: a brash, outspoken, and unconventional woman with one career (as a nightclub singer) already behind her. Bob dismisses Hazel in one early scene as "a tramp," but to contemporary audiences—who know what the postwar era holds, because they have lived it—she seems like someone ahead of her time, an emissary from a world that will be born after (and because of) the war. Kay and Hazel's friendship is, Denby argues, "a heroine sidekick relationship that is half forties movie, half-feminist paean to the glories of women's friendships."[20] Roger Ebert adds, "It's obvious the filmmakers didn't intend this as a movie about passion. Instead, it's about women in a man's world. . . . They also learn to support themselves, to think for themselves, and to see themselves differently. . . . This may be the first buddy movie about women."[21]

Mehlberg and Broderick agreed that they both had formed great and lasting friendships with the women they worked with, and that the film was very evocative of the period. The women left behind on the home front during the war learned to depend on each other—for support, for friendship, for counsel. Those who went to work in war industries built ships and planes and trucks and Jeeps, but they also built their own self-confidence, effective working relationships, and trust in each other. Though forced to return, in peacetime, to what society believed was their "natural" place in the home, they brought with them the lessons they had learned on the factory floor, and instilled in their daughters a sense of independence and self-confidence such that American women would never again sit on the sidelines.

Alice Kessler-Harris sees this reflected in the film: "If the film distorts the war and what women's lives were like during it, it occasionally manages to tell us something of the price women paid."[22] Toward the movie's end, the working women of the factory are treated to watching a film that extols the virtues of leaving work for the rewarding work of homemaking and child rearing. When Kay is laid off and is forced to hand in her leadman's shirt, she rebels slightly and tries to keep hold of her symbol of independence and accomplishment.

Historians have noted two distinct groups of "Rosies." On one hand, there were women who (like Anne Hilton in *Since You Went Away*) saw war work as a temporary detour from the customary roles of wife, mother, and homemaker. On the other hand, there were women who needed to work before, during, and after the war, and for whom "war production work was a move up in the labor force, not a temporary step out of the home."[23] Many of the latter group of women joined unions, learned valuable skills, and considered themselves permanent laborers in America's industrial realm: "Nearly three-quarters of all women interviewed, in government, union and public interests surveys wanted to retain their wartime jobs."[24] Kessler-Harris goes further, arguing that "virtually all 12 million [women] who had paying jobs before the war tried desperately to hang on to their well-paid work, bitterly resenting what they saw as a betrayal of their efforts."[25] These women were let go and forced, after the war, into more culturally acceptable feminine jobs as cooks, waitresses, and store clerks, but—as *New York Times* critic Vincent Canby observed—the first shots had been fired in the mid-twentieth century war for women's liberation.[26]

The scale of the social and cultural changes set in motion by World War II would not become fully apparent for decades. Even in the immediate postwar years, however, individual women were conscious that their lives had changed. Mehlberg noted that the female characters in Hollywood's home-front movies became much more independent and self-reliant than she did during the war, but she acknowledged that the war shaped her life, and is still a topic of conversation when she gathers with her peers. She believed that her war-year experiences even affected her own parenting style: she expected her own daughters to grow up as quickly as she had to and to demonstrate behavior far too mature for young girls of the postwar years. Broderick worked at the factory until the end of the war, when she was laid off. However when her husband returned from his war service, he had trouble finding work. Broderick learned that the factory was calling back some of the women who had worked there during the war, and family finances dictated that she go back. Eventually, their life stabilized; her husband began working in the building trades, retiring as a master pipefitter. A large picture of the USS *Corregidor* hung prominently on their living room wall for several years, a reminder of the war that—as Kay's husband Bob puts it in *Swing Shift*—made the whole world different.

These women are gone now, and the ranks of the "Rosies"—who wielded rivet guns and welding torches, circuit testers and micrometers in wartime factories—are thinning quickly, just as the ranks of uniformed World War II veterans are. The films of and about their generation are now among the best records we have of their wartime experience. These home-front films portray for new generations what life was like during the war. Broderick and Mehlberg, two members of the Greatest Generation, recognized the situations in the films: the rationing, the letter writing, the loneliness, and the work they took on . . . even as they recognized the dramatic license that Hollywood took in the interest of creating a better story, or more effective propaganda.

Since You Went Away and *Tender Comrade*, released during the war, were meant to be inspirational as well as entertaining. They modeled not only the expected behavior of those left at home during the war—cheerful acceptance of inconveniences like rationing, willingness to adapt to unconventional living and working arrangements, and stoic acceptance of personal loss—but also the ideals that patriotic Americans were expected to exhibit. With American involvement in the war framed as a great moral crusade (a war for democracy and against totalitarianism), "it was essential that the United States be seen practicing the ideals for which it claimed it was fighting."[27] Wartime propaganda, of which *Tender Comrade* and *Since You Went Away* are examples, was

> a conscious attempt to re-educate [American] citizens in the ideals which underpinned the Constitution and promote the unity necessary to wage total war. . . . These "lessons in democracy" came through a variety of forms . . . but most effectively through popular cinema. Film became the key weapon in the battle to re-educate America.[28]

Unknown to those who created it, it also helped to launch a social and cultural revolution that eventually transformed the lives of all American women.

CONCLUSION

The stories shared by these veterans and war workers offer us a glimpse of "personal histories" of World War II—each an insider's look at lives and times during a critical moment in American history, not typically found in history books or other formal texts—but they also offer something more. The veterans' memories, when placed in conversation with popular motion pictures, provides us with a new perspective on how history is portrayed in the movies. Despite historians' growing interest in film, many continue to dismiss all commercial motion pictures as purveyors of inaccurate "Hollywood history." As the preceding chapters have demonstrated, popular Hollywood films must address a different set of expectations in their narratives, and many of these expectations require the glossing or embellishing of historical detail—popular films have always had to shape their renditions of history to conform to budgets and available locations, as well as the interests and attention spans of their audiences—but as these veterans' stories and responses to the films have shown, not all Hollywood history is bad history.

The entry of the United States into World War II obliged Hollywood to stop focusing exclusively on mass entertainment and enter into a partnership with Washington to boost popular support for the war. The results of this partnership began appearing in the summer of 1942: a string of war propaganda films that began with *Wake Island* (1942) and continued through *Guadalcanal Diary* (1943), *Wing and a Prayer* (1944), and *Back to Bataan* (1945). These films not only mobilized America against the enemy and united the country in the war effort, but, according to such veterans as Lynn Simpson and James Hoisington, provided a surprisingly accurate portrait of what the war was like—what they themselves experienced while fighting the war in the Pacific. *The Memphis Belle* (1944), though based on footage shot in combat and nominally a documentary, was also part of Hollywood's wartime propaganda campaign employing William Wyler, one of Hollywood's most talented directors. Officially the chronicle of one plane, one crew, and one mission, it was a ringing tribute to all the Eighth Air Force crews that—going where ground forces could not yet reach—brought the war to the German homeland. Eighth Air Force veteran Jim Oberman lauded Wyler's film as an accurate record of the routine courage exhibited by the B-17 crews. Both in detail and in spirit, *The Memphis Belle* captured the experience of war fought tens of thousands of feet above enemy territory.

Oberman was equally complimentary about the 1949 film *Twelve O'Clock High*, which echoed *The Memphis Belle* both in its extensive use of actual combat footage and in its artful straddling of the boundary between fact and fiction, documentary and drama. An exploration of the psychological toll taken on soldiers by sustained combat, it was one of a cluster of films released in the years immediately after the war. Made when memories of the war were still fresh in the minds of filmmakers and audiences, but freed of the need to bolster public support for the war, these films offered an unprecedentedly gritty, realistic view of the war—a quality noted by veterans watching them decades later. Harry Miller, for example, recalled his involvement in the Battle of the Bulge and awarded *Battleground* (1949) high marks for accurately re-creating his wartime ordeal. *Sands of Iwo Jima*, released the same year, drew similar praise from Lynn Simpson for its portrayal of island-to-island fighting in the Pacific.

Hollywood's dedication to scrupulous historical accuracy and gritty realism may have been waning in the early 1960s, giving way to big-budget epics with all-star casts, but such films could also be accurate portraits of the war. According to World War II veteran Ernest Thorp, the Hollywood big-budget extravaganza *The Great Escape* (1963) was both a factual and faithful account of the real (historical) Great Escape from Stalag Luft III, the Luftwaffe-run prisoner-of-war camp where Thorp was imprisoned for nine months. The film brought back memories for Thorp, including small, long-forgotten details, from the ingenuity of prisoners who scrounged, sewed, and manufactured escape equipment to the details of an informal barter economy in which cigarettes and chocolate bars were like silver and gold. *The Great Escape* also recalled, for Thorp, the attitudes of his fellow POWs toward confinement: the Americans' optimism that the war would soon be over, the Brits' seemingly playful (yet deadly serious) attitude toward escaping, and the desperate desire for freedom that drove men "round the bend" after too many years spent behind the wire.

To a man, the former soldiers' memories of their time in combat had not been dimmed nor these memories clouded by the passage of decades. They still recall in vivid detail the time when—as young men (boys, really)—they were sent by their country to fight in foreign lands, defeat the most-feared armies on earth, and defend democracy and the ideals that Americans of their era held dear. The silver-screen heroes in wartime films promoted those ideals through patriotic speeches, but they also modeled them in their behavior. Hollywood's infantry squads, bomber crews, and ship's companies—diverse in their ethnic heritages, class backgrounds, and regional accents, but united by a common goal and unswerving loyalty to one another—embodied the motto *E pluribus unum*. The tenacity with which John Wayne's Filipino guerillas resisted the enemy in *Back to Bataan*, the daring with which Dana Andrews's pilots pressed home their attacks in *Wing and a Prayer*, and the ingenuity with which Claudette Colbert responded to the hardships of war on the home front in *Since You Went Away* showed Americans at their best.

The films of the postwar era, though darker in tone, continued the trend. Sergeant Kinnie in *Battleground* may be on the verge of physical collapse, and General Savage in *Twelve O'Clock High* may be on the verge of mental breakdown, but they remain exemplary American leaders: fierce in battle, but deeply concerned about the well-being of their men during the quiet moments before and after. The two principal American characters in *The Great Escape*—Hendley, "the Scrounger" (James Garner), and Hilts, "the Cooler King" (Steve McQueen)—may be bigger than life, but they are bigger in distinctly *American* ways. They are determined loners, brilliant improvisers, and always ready to mock the self-important and challenge the powerful. Once outside the wire, they make the film's most spectacular escape attempts: stealing a plane (Hendley) and a motorcycle (Hilts) in their desperate race for the Swiss frontier. Both scenes are invented—"Hollywood moments" to thrill the audience—but in a deeper sense they are "true." They reflect the audacity and outsized dreams that defined the "Greatest Generation," and shaped their approach to war.

Whether more recent films, separated from the war by decades rather than years, can capture history as effectively is up for debate. Films like *Swing Shift* (1984) and the fictionalized *Memphis Belle* (1990) have been criticized for getting the look of the period right, but the rhythms of life on the home front and the battlefield significantly wrong. Thomas Begay, who as a Navajo code talker witnessed some of the most brutal fighting of the war, called *Windtalkers* (2002), Hollywood's recent attempt to tell the code talkers' story, "a bunch of lies." Historians' understanding of World War II as an event has improved with the passage of time; Hollywood's ability to depict it plausibly on-screen may have moved in the opposite direction.

Historians today continue to debate the role that Hollywood film should play in the study of history. Andrew Bergman has argued that the Hollywood productions of the 1930s revealed much about this country and its people during the Great Depression.[1] He contends that Hollywood gave America what it desperately wanted and needed in order to survive the realities of that decade. A careful viewing of William Wyler's *The Best Years of Our Lives* (1946) reveals a film that, in its day, was considered to be a painfully accurate depiction of the problems returning American veterans faced in their first weeks and months at home. Today, for audiences looking back and trying to understand, the film can still play that role. Similarly, Peter Biskind, in his study of several films produced in Hollywood during the 1950s,[2] has demonstrated that these productions clearly reflected the American values, attitudes, hopes, and fears that were manifested during a decade that simultaneously reinforced the status quo and sowed the seeds of the social and cultural revolution that crested in the 1960s.

Historian Robert Rosenstone acknowledges a point raised by critics of historical film: that, indeed, presenting history on film rather than on the page requires adjustments and compromises.[3] He concludes, however, that these do not necessarily produce poor history. The filmmaker's need to infuse historical events with color, sound, and action can pay benefits, since it enables him or her to immerse viewers in the time and place being re-created on-screen. The written word may offer greater subtlety, and the still photograph greater accuracy, but only films—or, rather, only *good* films—allow us to briefly inhabit the past. Only film allows us to simultaneously view landscapes, hear sounds, and experience the flavor of a particular historical site or event.

The youngest remaining veterans of World War II—the last eyewitnesses to the greatest war of the twentieth century—are nearly ninety. Before long, our last chance to ask them, "What was it like?" will be gone. Hollywood's re-creations of the war cannot replace the recollections of those who lived through it, but—as the interviews collected in this book suggest—they may, if viewed thoughtfully, offer an important window on one of the defining moments in modern history.

FILMOGRAPHY

Back to Bataan (1945, RKO Radio Pictures)

Director: Edward Dmytryk
Screenplay: Ben Barzman
Producers: Robert Fellows and Theron Warth
Music: Roy Webb; Cinematography: Nicholas Musuraca; Editing: Marston Fay
Specs: 95 minutes; black and white
Cast: John Wayne (Col. Joseph Madden); Anthony Quinn (Capt. Andrés Bonifácio); Beulah Bondi (Bertha Barnes); Fely Franquelli (Dalisay Delgado)
Summary: After the fall of the Philippines to the Japanese in World War II, Col. Joseph Madden of the U.S. Army stays on to organize guerrilla fighters against the conquerors.
Availability: DVD (Turner Home Entertainment)

Battleground (1949, MGM)

Director: William Wellman
Screenplay: Robert Pirosh
Producer: Samuel Goldwyn
Music: Lennie Hayton; Cinematography: Paul C. Vogel; Editing: John Dunning
Specs: 118 minutes; black and white

Cast: Van Johnson (Holley), John Hodiak (Jarvess), Ricardo Montalban (Roderigues), George Murphy (Stazak), Marshall Thompson
(Layton), James Whitmore (Kinnie)
Summary: A squad of soldiers from the 101st Airborne Division, low
on food and ammunition, struggles to keep Bastogne out of German hands during the Battle of the Bulge.
Availability: DVD (Warner Home Video)

The Battle of the Bulge (1965, Warner Bros.)

Director: Ken Annakin
Screenplay: Philip Yordan, Milton Sperling, and John Melton
Producers: Milton Sperling and Philip Yordan
Music: Benjamin Frankel; Cinematography: Jack Hildyard; Editing:
Eugène Lourié
Specs: 167 minutes; color
Cast: Henry Fonda (Lt. Col. Dan Kiley), Robert Shaw (Col. Kessler),
Robert Ryan (Gen. Grey), Dana Andrews (Col. Pritchard), George
Montgomery (Sgt. Duquesne), James MacArthur (Lt. Weaver),
Telly Savalas (Sgt. Guffy)
Summary: American forces struggle to regroup after the German army
launches a massive surprise attack in the Ardennes region of Bel-
gium a few weeks before Christmas, 1944.
Availability: DVD (Warner Home Video); Blu-ray (Warner Home
Video)

The Best Years of Our Lives (1946, The Samuel Goldwyn Company)

Director: William Wyler
Screenplay: Robert E. Sherwood (from the novel by MacKinlay Kan-
tor)
Producer: Samuel Goldwyn
Music: Hugo Friedhofer; Cinematography: Gregg Toland; Editing:
Daniel Mandell
Specs: 172 minutes; color
Cast: Myrna Loy (Milly Stephens), Fredric March (Al Stephens),
Dana Andrews (Fred Derry), Teresa Wright (Peggy Stephens), Vir-
ginia Mayo (Marie Derry), Harold Russell (Homer Parrish)

Summary: Three postwar lives of three demobilized veterans from the same town intersect as they struggle to readapt to civilian life and reconnect with the loved ones they left behind.
Availability: DVD (MGM); Blu-ray (Warner Home Video)

A Bridge Too Far (1978, United Artists)

Director: Richard Attenborough
Screenplay: William Goldman (based on the book by Cornelius Ryan)
Producer: Joseph E. Levine
Music: John Addison; Cinematography: Geoffrey Unsworth; Editing: Antony Gibbs
Specs: 178 minutes; color
Cast: Dirk Bogarde (Lt. Gen. Frederik "Boy" Browning), Sean Connery (Maj. Gen. Roy Urquhart), Gene Hackman (Maj. Gen. Stanislaw Sosabowski), Ryan O'Neal (Brig. Gen. James Gavin), Michael Caine (Lt. Col. J.O.E. Vandaleur), Robert Redford (Maj. Julian Cook)
Summary: A re-creation of Operation Market Garden (September 1944), a daring but unsuccessful Allied plan to seize several key bridges over the Lower Rhine and its tributaries with airborne and armored forces, encircling retreating German forces and ending the war by Christmas.
Availability: DVD (United Artists); Blu-ray (MGM)

The Fighting Seabees (1944, Republic Pictures)

Director: Edward Ludwig
Screenplay: Borden Chase
Producer: Albert J. Cohen
Music: Walter Scharf; Cinematography: William Bradford; Editing: Richard L. Van Enger
Specs: 100 minutes; black and white
Cast: John Wayne (Lt. Cmdr. Wedge Donovan); Susan Hayward (Constance Chesley); Dennis O'Keefe (Lt. Cmdr. Robert Yarrow); William Frawley (Eddie Powers)
Summary: Construction workers in World War II in the Pacific are needed to build military sites, but the work is dangerous and they

doubt the ability of the Navy to protect them. After a series of attacks by the Japanese, something new is tried: Construction Battalions (CBs, or Seabees). The new Seabees have to both build and be ready to fight.

Availability: DVD (Olive Films); Blu-ray (Olive Films)

Flying Leathernecks (1951, RKO Radio Pictures)

Director: Nicholas Ray
Screenplay: James Edward Grant
Producer: Edmund Grainger
Music: Roy Webb; Cinematography: William E. Snyder; Editing: Sherman Todd
Specs: 102 minutes; color
Cast: John Wayne (Maj. Daniel Xavier Kirby); Robert Ryan (Capt. Carl "Griff" Griffin); Don Taylor (Lt. Vern "Cowboy" Blithe); Janis Carter (Joan Kirby)
Summary: Major Kirby leads the Wildcats squadron into the historic battle of Guadalcanal.
Availability: DVD (Turner Home Entertainment)

Flying Tigers (1942, Republic Pictures)

Director: David Miller
Screenplay: Kenneth Gamet
Producer: Edmund Grainger
Music: Victor Young; Cinematography: Jack A. Marta; Editing: Ernest J. Nims
Specs: 102 minutes; black and white
Cast: John Wayne (Capt. Jim Gordon); John Carroll (Woody Jason); Anna Lee (Brooke Elliott); Paul Kelly (Hap Smith)
Summary: Capt. Jim Gordon's command of the famed American mercenary fighter group in China is complicated by the recruitment of an old friend who is a reckless hotshot.
Availability: DVD (Republic Pictures); Blu-ray (Olive Films)

A Foreign Affair (1948, Paramount)

Director: Billy Wilder

Screenplay: Charles Brackett, Billy Wilder, and Richard L. Breen
Producer: Charles Brackett
Music: Friedrich Hollaender; Cinematography: Charles Lang; Editing: Doane Harrison
Specs: 116 minutes; black and white
Cast: Jean Arthur (Phoebe Frost), Marlene Dietrich (Erika Von Schluetow), John Lund (Capt. John Pringle), Millard Mitchell (Col. Rufus J. Plummer), Peter von Zerneck (Hans Otto Birgel)
Summary: Political satire about a U.S. Congresswoman who travels to occupied Berlin to investigate rumors of corruption, not realizing that the Army officer she enlists to assist her is romantically involved with a German lounge singer tied to a Nazi war criminal
Availability: DVD (Universal Home Video/Turner Classic Movies)

Foreign Correspondent (1940, Walter Wanger Productions)

Director: Alfred Hitchcock
Screenplay: Charles Bennett and Joan Harrison
Producer: Walter Wanger
Music: Alfred Newman; Cinematography: Rudolph Maté; Editing: Dorothy Spencer
Specs: 120 minutes; black and white
Cast: Joel McCrea (Johnny Jones), Larraine Day (Carol Fisher), Herbert Marshall (Stephen Fisher), George Sanders (ffolliott), Albert Basserman (Van Meer)
Summary: On the eve of World War II, a naive but tenacious American reporter is sent to Europe as a foreign correspondent, and becomes involved with assassination, espionage, and political intrigue.
Availability: DVD (Warner Home Video); Blu-ray (Criterion Collection)

The Great Dictator (1940, Charles Chaplin Productions)

Director: Charles Chaplin
Screenplay: Charles Chaplin
Producer: Charles Chaplin

Music: Charles Chaplin and Meredith Wilson; Cinematography: Karl Struss and Roland Totheroh; Editing: Willard Nico

Specs: 125 minutes; black and white

Cast: Charles Chaplin (Adenoid Hynkel, Dictator of Tomania/A Jewish Barber), Jack Oakie (Napaloni, Dictator of Bacteria), Reginald Gardiner (Schultz), Henry Daniell (Garbitsch), Paulette Goddard (Hannah)

Summary: In a thinly disguised satire of Hitler and Nazism, dictator Adenoid Hynkel pursues ruthless policies designed to rid Tomainia of Jews and turn it into a pure Aryan state, while a Jewish barber struggles to survive under his regime.

Availability: DVD (Criterion Collection); Blu-ray (Criterion Collection)

The Great Escape (1963, The Mirisch Company)

Director: John Sturges

Screenplay: James Clavell and W. R. Burnett, based on the book by Paul Brickhill

Producer: John Sturges

Music: Elmer Bernstein; Cinematography: Daniel L. Fapp; Editing: Ferris Webster

Specs: 172 minutes; color

Cast: Steve McQueen (Hilts, "the Cooler King"), James Garner (Hendley, "the Scrounger"), Richard Attenborough (Bartlett), James Donald (Ramsey), Charles Bronson (Danny, "the Tunnel King"), Donald Pleasance (Blythe), James Coburn (Sedgwick), David McCallum (Ashley-Pitt)

Summary: Prisoner-of-war drama featuring primarily British POWs, along with a handful of Americans.

Availability: DVD (Fox Searchlight); Blu-ray (Fox Searchlight)

Guadalcanal Diary (1943, 20th Century Fox)

Director: Lewis Seller

Screenplay: Lamar Trotti and Jerome Cady, based on the book by Richard Tregaskis

Producer: Bryan Foy

Music: David Buttolph; Cinematography: Charles Clarke; Editing: Fred Allen

Specs: 93 minutes; black and white

Cast: Preston Foster (Father Donnelly), Lloyd Nolan (Sgt. "Hook" Malone), William Bendix (Cpl. Aloysius "Taxi" Potts), Richard Conte (Capt. Davis), Anthony Quinn (Jesus "Soose" Alvarez), Richard Jaeckel (Johnny "Chicken" Anderson)

Summary: A U.S. Army infantry unit fights against overwhelming odds to hold the strategic South Pacific Island of Guadalcanal against the Japanese in 1942.

Availability: DVD (20th Century Fox)

Inglourious Basterds (2009, Universal Studios)

Director: Quentin Tarantino

Screenplay: Quentin Tarantino

Producer: Lawrence Bender

Music: Francesco De Masi; Cinematography: Giovanni Bergamini; Editing: Gianfranco Amicucci

Specs: 153 minutes; color

Cast: Brad Pitt (Lt. Aldo Raine), Mélanie Laurent (Shosanna), Christoph Waitz (Col. Hans Landa), Diane Kruger (Bridget von Hammersmark), Eli Roth (Sgt. Donny Donowitz), Michael Fassbender (Lt. Archie Hicox)

Summary: In Nazi-occupied France, a young Jewish woman's plans for revenge on the German officer who murdered her family intersect with the mission of a ruthless group of Jewish American commandos.

Availability: DVD (Universal Studios); Blu-ray (Universal Studios)

The Longest Day (1962, Daryl F. Zanuck Productions/20th Century Fox)

Director: Ken Annakin, Andrew Marton, Bernhard Wicki

Screenplay: Cornelius Ryan, based on his book

Producer: Daryl F. Zanuck

Music: Maurice Jarre; Cinematography: Jean Bourgoin and Walter Wottitz; Editing: Samuel E. Beetley

Specs: 178 minutes; black and white

Cast: John Wayne (Lt. Col. Benjamin Vandevoort), Robert Ryan (Brig. Gen. James Gavin), Henry Fonda (Brig. Gen. Theodore Roosevelt, Jr.), Red Buttons (Pvt. John Steele), Richard Todd (Maj. John Howard), Peter Lawford (Lord Lovat), Cürt Jurgens (Gen. Gunther Blumentritt), Robert Mitchum (Brig. Gen. Norman Cota), Paul Hartman (Field Marshall Gerd von Rundstedt)

Summary: An all-star cast and three directors (one American, one British, and one German) re-create the invasion of Normandy on June 6, 1944.

Availability: DVD (20th Century Fox); Blu-ray (20th Century Fox)

The Memphis Belle: A Story of a Flying Fortress (1944, First Motion Picture Unit, U.S. Army Air Forces)

Director: William Wyler

Screenplay: Jerome Chodorov, Lester Koenig, William Wyler

Music: Gail Kubik; Cinematography: William H. Clothier, William V. Skall, Harold J. Tannenbaum, and William Wyler; Editing: William Wyler

Specs: 43 minutes; color

Cast: Col. Stanley Wray (himself), Capt. Robert Morgan (himself), Capt. James A. Verinis (himself), Sgt. Robert J. Hanson (himself), Capt. Chuck Leighton (himself), Sgt. Harold Loch (himself)

Summary: Documentary cameras follow the crew of the B-17 bomber *Memphis Belle* on the twenty-fifth and final mission of their tour, a raid on the submarine pens at Wilhelmshafen, Germany.

Availability: DVD (Echo Bridge Home Entertainment); Blu-ray (Periscope Film)

Memphis Belle (1990, Enigma Productions/Warner Bros.)

Director: Michael Caton-Jones

Screenplay: Monte Merrick

Producers: David Puttnam and Catherine Wyler

Specs: 107 minutes; color

Cast: Matthew Modine (Capt. Dennis Dearborn), Eric Stolz (Sgt. Danny Daly), Tate Donovan (Lt. Luke Sinclair), D. B. Sweeney (Lt.

Phil Lowenthal), Billy Zane (Lt. Valentine "Val" Kozlowski), Sean Astin (Sgt. Richard "Rascal" Moore)

Summary: In a heavily fictionalized remake of William Wyler's wartime documentary, the crew of a B-17 bomber encounters a series of crises during the twenty-fifth and final mission of their combat tour.

Availability: DVD (Warner Home Video); Blu-ray (Warner Home Video)

Midway (1976, Universal Studios)

Director: Jack Smight

Screenplay: Donald S. Sanford

Producer: Walter Mirisch

Music: John Williams; Cinematography: Harry Stradling Jr.; Editing: Robert Swink and Frank J. Urioste

Specs: 132 minutes; color

Cast: Charlton Heston (Capt. Matt Garth), Henry Fonda (Adm. Chester Nimitz), James Coburn (Capt. Vinton Maddox), Glenn Ford (Rear Adm. Raymond Spruance), Hal Holbrook (Cmdr. Joseph Rochefort), Toshiro Mifune (Adm. Isoroku Yamamoto)

Summary: The Japanese navy attacks Midway Island, unaware that the Americans can read their coded messages and that the carriers of the U.S. Pacific Fleet are waiting for them, setting the stage for a battle that will change the course of the war.

Availability: DVD (Universal Studios); Blu-ray (Universal Studios)

The Mortal Storm (1940, Metro-Goldwyn-Mayer)

Director: Frank Borzage

Screenplay: Claudine West and Hans Rameau

Producers: Frank Borzage and Victor Saville

Music: Edward Kane; Cinematography: William H. Daniels; Editing: Elmo Veron

Specs: 100 minutes; black and white

Cast: Margaret Sullavan (Freya Roth); James Stewart (Martin Breitner); Robert Young (Fritz Marberg); Frank Morgan (Professor Roth)

Summary: The Roth family lead a quiet life in a small village in the German Alps during the early 1930s. When the Nazis come to power, the family is divided and Martin Brietner, a family friend, is caught up in the turmoil.
Availability: DVD (MGM)

Mrs. Miniver (1942, MGM)

Director: William Wyler
Screenplay: Arthur Wimperis, George Froeschel, James Hilton, and Claudine West (based on the novel by Jan Struther)
Producers: Sidney Franklin and William Wyler
Music: Herbert Stothart; Cinematography: Joseph Ruttneberg; Editing: Harold F. Kress
Specs: 132 minutes; black and white
Cast: Greer Garson (Kay Miniver), Walter Pidgeon (Clem Miniver), Teresa Wright (Carol Beldon), Dame May Whitty (Lady Beldon), Reginald Owen (Foley), Henry Travers (Mr. Ballard)
Summary: The story of an average middle-class family in a small English village from the summer of 1939 through the London Blitz of 1941, "doing their bit" as Britain stands alone against the Nazis.
Availability: DVD (Warner Home Video); Blu-ray (Warner Home Video)

Patton (1970, 20th Century Fox)

Director: Franklin J. Schaffner
Screenplay: Francis Ford Coppola and Edwin H. North
Producer: Frank McCarthy
Music: Jerry Goldsmith; Cinematography: Fred Koenekamp; Editing: Hugh S. Fowler
Specs: 172 minutes; color
Cast: George C. Scott (Gen. George S. Patton), Karl Malden (Gen. Omar N. Bradley), Stephen Young (Capt. Chester B. Hansen), Karl Michael Vogler (Field Marshall Erwin Rommel), Michael Bates (Field Marshall Bernard Law Montgomery)
Summary: The World War II career of General George Patton, whose aggressive tactics, enthusiasm for battle, and prickly personality

made him America's most effective—and most controversial—wartime general.

Availability: DVD (Fox Searchlight); Blu-ray (Fox Searchlight)

Pearl Harbor (2001, Buena Vista)

Director: Michael Bay

Screenplay: Randall Wallace

Producers: Michael Bay and Jerry Bruckheimer

Music: Hans Zimmer; Cinematography: John Schwartzman; Editing: Roger Barton, Mark Goldblatt, Chris Lebenson, and Steven Rosenblum

Specs: 183 minutes; color

Cast: Ben Affleck (Capt. Rafe McCawley), Josh Hartnett (Capt. Danny Walker), Kate Beckinsale (Lt. Evelyn Johnson), Alec Baldwin (Lt. Col. James Doolittle), Jon Voight (Franklin D. Roosevelt)

Summary: During the early years of World War II, two childhood friends join the Army Air Forces and fight in a series of pivotal early battles—including the attack on Pearl Harbor—while pursuing the same woman.

Availability: DVD (Buena Vista Home Entertainment); Blu-ray (Buena Vista Home Entertainment)

Sahara (1943, Columbia)

Director: Zoltan Korda

Screenplay: John Howard Lawson and Zoltan Korda

Producer: Harry Joe Brown

Music: Miklos Rozsa; Cinematography: Rudolph Maté; Editing: Charles Nugent

Specs: 97 minutes; black and white

Cast: Humphrey Bogart (Sgt. Joe Gunn), Bruce Bennett (Waco Hoyt), J. Carroll Naish (Giuseppe), Lloyd Bridges (Fred Clarkson), Rex Ingram (Sgt. Maj. Tambul), Richard Aherne (Capt. Jason Halliday)

Summary: After the fall of Tobruk, the crew of a lone American tank traverses the Libyan desert, joined by British, French, and Sudanese soldiers and German and Italian prisoners as it searches for badly needed water.

Availability: DVD (Sony Pictures Home Entertainment)

Sands of Iwo Jima (1949, Republic Pictures)

Director: Allan Dwan
Screenplay: James Edward Grant
Producer: Edmund Grainger
Music: Victor Young; Cinematography: Reggie Lanning; Editing:
   Richard L. Van Enger
Specs: 100 minutes; black and white
Cast: John Wayne (Sgt. John Stryker); John Agar (Pfc. Peter Con-
   way); Adele Mara (Allison Bromley); Forrest Tucker (Pfc. Al
   Thomas)
Summary: A dramatization of the Battle of Iwo Jima.
Availability: DVD (Republic Pictures); Blu-ray (Olive Films)

Saving Private Ryan (1998, Paramount)

Director: Stephen Spielberg
Screenplay: Robert Rodat
Producers: Allison Lyon Segon, Bonnie Curtis, Gary Levinson, Ian
   Bryce, and Kevin De La Noy
Music: John Williams; Cinematography: Janusz Kaminski; Editing:
   Michael Kahn
Specs: 169 minutes; color
Cast: Tom Hanks (Capt. John Miller), Matt Damon (Pvt. James Fran-
   cis Ryan), Tom Sizemore (Sgt. Mike Horvath), Edward Burns (Pvt.
   Richard Reiben), Barry Pepper (Pvt. Daniel Jackson), Vin Diesel
   (Pvt. Adrian Caparzo), Adam Goldberg (Pvt. Stanley Mellish)
Summary: In the chaos following the D-Day invasion, a squad of U.S.
   Rangers is sent into the French countryside to locate and bring
   back Private James Ryan, a paratrooper who has been ordered
   home because his four brothers have all been killed in action.
Availability: DVD (Dreamworks Video); Blu-ray (Paramount)

Since You Went Away (1944, MGM)

Director: John Cromwell, Edward Cline (uncredited)

Screenplay: David O. Selznick and Margaret Buell Wilder, based on
the book by Margaret Buell Wilder
Producer: David O. Selznick
Music: Max Steiner; Cinematography: Stanley Cortez; Editing: John
Faure
Specs: 177 minutes; black and white
Cast: Claudette Colbert (Anne Hilton), Jennifer Jones (Jane Hilton),
Joseph Cotten (Lt. Tony Willet), Shirley Temple (Bridget Hilton),
Monty Woolley (Col. William Smollett)
Summary: Anne Hilton copes with shortages and rationing on the
home front while her husband is at war, and takes in a lodger,
Colonel Smollett, to help make ends meet.
Availability: DVD (MGM)

So Proudly We Hail! (1943, Paramount Pictures)

Director: Mark Sandrich
Screenplay: Alan Scott
Producer: Mark Sandrich
Music: Miklós Rózsa; Cinematography: Charles Lang; Editing: Ells-
worth Hoagland
Specs: 126 minutes; black and white
Cast: Claudette Colbert (Lt. Janet "Davy" Davidson), Paulette God-
dard (Lt. Joan O'Doul), Veronica Lake (Lt. Olivia D'Arcy),
George Reeves (Lt. John Summers)
Summary: A group of U.S. Army nurses leaves San Francisco for their
tour of duty in Hawaii in December 1941. The attack on Pearl
Harbor changes their destination, and their lives.
Availability: DVD (Universal Studios)

Stalag 17 (1953, Paramount Pictures)

Director: Billy Wilder
Screenplay: Billy Wilder and Edwin Blum
Producers: Billy Wilder and William Schorr
Music: Franz Waxman; Cinematography: Ernest Laszlo; Editing:
George Tomasini
Specs: 120 minutes; black and white

Cast: William Holden (Sgt. J. J. Sefton), Don Taylor (Lt. James Dunbar), Otto Preminger (Obert von Scherbach), Robert Strauss (Sgt. Stanislaus "Animal" Kuzawa)

Summary: When two escaping American World War II prisoners are killed, the German POW camp barracks black marketeer, J. J. Sefton, is suspected of being an informer.

Availability: DVD (Paramount); Blu-ray (Paramount)

The Story of G.I. Joe (1945, Lester Cowan Productions)

Director: William Wellman

Screenplay: Leopold Atlas, Guy Endore, and Philip Stevenson

Producers: David Hall and Lester Cowan

Music: Louis Applebaum and Ann Ronell; Cinematography: Russell Metty; Editing: Albrecht Joseph

Specs: 108 minutes; black and white

Cast: Burgess Meredith (Ernie Pyle), Robert Mitchum (Lt. Walker), Freddie Steele (Sgt. Warnicki), Wally Cassell (Pvt. Dondaro), Jimmy Lloyd (Pvt. Spencer)

Summary: Newspaper reporter Ernie Pyle wins the respect and admiration of American soldiers by living with them at the front in North Africa and Italy, sharing their hardships, and writing stories that describe the war from their perspective.

Availability: DVD (Image Entertainment)

Swing Shift (1984, Warner Bros.)

Director: Jonathan Demme

Screenplay: Nancy Dowd

Producer: Jerry Bick

Music: Patrick Williams; Cinematography: Tak Fujimoto; Editing: Gib Jaffe, Craig McKay

Specs: 100 minutes; color

Cast: Goldie Hawn (Kay Walsh); Kurt Russell (Mike "Lucky" Lockhart); Christine Lahti (Hazel); Fred Ward (Archibald "Biscuits" Toule); Ed Harris (Jack Walsh)

Summary: In 1941, Jack Walsh enlists after Pearl Harbor. Against his wishes, his wife takes a job at the local aircraft plant where she

meets Hazel, a singer. The two soon become fast friends and also increasingly expert workers.
Availability: DVD (Warner Home Video)

Tender Comrade (1943, RKO Radio Pictures)

Director: Edward Dmytryk
Screenplay: Dalton Trumbo
Producers: David Hempstead and Sherman Todd
Music: Leigh Harline; Cinematography: Russell Metty; Editing: Roland Gross
Specs: 102 minutes; black and white
Cast: Ginger Rogers (Jo Jones), Robert Ryan (Chris Jones), Ruth Hussey (Barbara Thomas), Patricia Collinge (Helen Stacey)
Summary: A young defense plant worker whose husband is in the military during World War II shares a house with three other women in the same situation.
Availability: VHS (Warner Home Video)

They Were Expendable (1945, Metro-Goldwyn-Mayer)

Director: John Ford, Robert Montgomery (uncredited)
Screenplay: Frank Wead, based on the book by William L. White
Producer: Cliff Reid, John Ford (uncredited)
Music: Herbert Stothart; Cinematography: Joseph H. August; Editing: Douglass Biggs and Frank E. Hull
Specs: 135 minutes; black and white
Cast: Robert Montgomery (Lt. John Brickley), John Wayne (Lt. j.g. "Rusty" Ryan), Donna Reed (Lt. Sandy Davyss), Jack Holt (Gen. Martin)
Summary: A dramatized account of the role of the U.S. PT boats in the defense of the Philippines in World War II.
Availability: DVD (Warner Home Video)

Tora! Tora! Tora! (1970, 20th Century Fox/Toei Company)

Directors: Richard Fleischer, Kinji Fukasaku, and Toshio Masuda
Screenplay: Larry Forrester, Hideo Oguni, and Ryuzo Kikushima
Producers: Richard Fleischer and Elmo Williams

Music: Jerry Goldsmith; Cinematography: Osami Furuya, Sinsaku
Hameda, Masamichi Sato, and Charles F. Wheeler; Editing: Pem-
broke J. Herring, Shinya Inoue, and James E. Newcom
Specs: 144 minutes; color
Cast: Martin Balsam (Adm. Husband Kimmel), Soh Yamamura
(Adm. Isoroku Yamamoto), Joseph Cotton (Henry Stimson), Tat-
suya Mihashi (Cmdr. Minoru Genda), E. G. Marshall (Lt. Col.
Brandon), Takahiro Tamura (Lt. Cmdr. Mitsuo Fuchida), James
Whitmore (Adm. William Halsey)
Summary: A semi-documentary retelling of the Japanese attack on
Pearl Harbor from both sides of the battle—written, directed, and
photographed by a joint Japanese and American crew.
Availability: DVD (Fox Searchlight); Blu-ray (Fox Searchlight)

True Whispers: The Story of the Navajo Code Talkers (2002, Red Horse
Productions)

Director: Valerie Red-Horse
Screenplay: Valerie Red-Horse
Producer: Valerie Red-Horse
Specs: 57 minutes; color
Cast: William H. Macy (Narrator)
Summary: Documentary telling the story of the Navajo code talkers
who fought in World War II.
Availability: DVD (PBS)

Twelve O'Clock High (1949, 20th Century Fox)

Director: Henry King
Screenplay: Sy Bartlett and Beirnie Lay, Jr.
Producer: Daryl F. Zanuck
Music: Alfred Newman; Cinematography: Leon Shamroy; Editing:
Barbara McLean
Specs: 132 minutes; black and white
Cast: Gregory Peck (Brig. Gen. Frank Savage), Hugh Marlowe (Lt.
Col. Ben Gately), Gary Merrill (Col. Keith Davenport), Dean Jag-
ger (Maj. Harvey Stovall), Millard Mitchell (Maj. Gen. Ben Pritch-
ard), Robert Arthur (Sgt. McIlhenny)

Summary: In 1942, a tough-minded Army Air Forces general takes command of a "hard-luck" bomber group and attempts to restore its crews' combat effectiveness and sense of pride; he succeeds, but at a terrible personal cost.

Availability: DVD (Fox Searchlight); Blu-ray (20th Century Fox)

U-571 (2000, Universal)

Director: Jonathan Mostow

Screenplay: Jonathan Mostow, Sam Montgomery, and David Ayer

Producers: Dino De Laurentis and Martha De Laurentis

Music: Richard Marvin; Cinematography: Oliver Wood; Editing: Wayne Wahrman

Specs: 116 minutes; color

Cast: Matthew McConaughey (Lt. Andrew Tyler), Bill Paxton (Lt. Cmdr. Mike Dhalgren), Harvey Keitel (CPO Henry Klough), Jon Bon Jovi (Lt. Pete Emmett), David Keith (Capt. Matthew Coonan), Thomas Kretschmer (Capt. Lt. Gunther Wassner)

Summary: The crew of an American submarine boards a crippled German U-boat in order to steal its top-secret Enigma coding machine, but must fight for their lives when they become trapped on the enemy vessel.

Availability: DVD (Universal Studios); Blu-ray (Universal Studios)

Wake Island (1942, Paramount)

Director: John Farrow

Screenplay: W. R. Burnett and Frank Butler

Producer: Joseph Sistrom

Music: David Buttolph; Cinematography: William C. Mello and Theodor Sparkuhl; Editing: Frank Bracht and LeRoy Stone

Specs: 87 minutes; black and white

Cast: Brian Donlevy (Maj. Geoffrey Caton), MacDonald Carey (Lt. Bruce Cameron), Robert Preston (Pvt. Joe Doyle), William Bendix (Pvt. Aloysius "Smacksie" Randall), Albert Dekker (Shad McCloskey)

Summary: After Pearl Harbor, a small Navy and Marine garrison with no hope of reinforcement or resupply makes a heroic last stand against a Japanese invasion of their strategic Pacific island.
Availability: DVD (Universal Studios)

Windtalkers (2002, Metro-Goldwyn-Mayer)

Director: John Woo
Screenplay: John Rice and Joe Batteer
Producers: Terence Chang, Tracie Graham-Rice, Alison R. Rosenzweig, John Woo
Music: James Horner; Cinematography: Jeffrey L. Kimball; Editing: Jeff Gullo, Steven Kemper, and Tom Rolf
Specs: 134 minutes; color
Cast: Nicholas Cage (Sgt. Joe Enders); Adam Beach (Pvt. Ben Yahzee); Peter Stormare (Gunnery Sgt. Hjelmstad); Noah Emmerich (Private Chick)
Summary: During World War II when the Americans needed a secure method of communicating, a code was devised using the Navajo language. Navajos were recruited to become what would be known as code talkers.
Availability: DVD (Fox Searchlight); Blu-ray (MGM)

Wing and a Prayer (1944, 20th Century Fox)

Director: Henry Hathaway
Screenplay: Jerome Cady, Jo Swerling, Mortimer Braus
Producers: Walter Morosco, William A. Bacher
Music: Hugo W. Friedhofer; Cinematography: Glen MacWilliams; Editing: J. Watson Webb
Specs: 97 minutes; black and white
Cast: Don Ameche (Cmdr. Bingo Harper), Dana Andrews (Lt. Cmdr. Edward Moulton), William Eythe (Ens. Hallam "Oscar" Scott), Charles Bickford (Capt. Waddell), Kevin O'Shea (Ens. Charles "Cookie" Cunningham), Richard Jaeckel ("Beezy" Bessemer)
Summary: After Pearl Harbor, a lone aircraft carrier crisscrosses the Pacific on a secret mission to deceive the Japanese and lure them into a trap at Midway.

Availability: DVD (20th Century Fox)

A Yank in the RAF (1941, 20th Century Fox)

Director: Henry King
Screenplay: Darryl F. Zanuck, Darrell Ware, and Karl Tunberg
Producers: Darryl F. Zanuck and Louis F. Edelman
Music: Alfred Newman; Cinematography: Leon Shamroy; Editing:
    Barbara McLean
Specs: 98 minutes; black and white
Cast: Tyrone Power (Tim Baker), Betty Grable (Carol Brown), John
    Sutton (Wing Cmdr. Morley), Reginald Gardener (Roger Pillby),
    Donald Stuart (Cpl. Harry Baker), Ralph Byrd (Al Bennett)
Summary: A hotshot American pilot finds himself in London in 1940,
    falls for a chorus girl, and joins the Royal Air Force in order to be
    near her, only to find himself competing with his superior officer
    for her affections.
Availability: DVD (20th Century Fox)

NOTES

1. HOLLYWOOD, HISTORY, AND THE HISTORIAN

1. Peter C. Rollins, personal interview, February 5, 1997.
2. Bergman, *We're in the Money*, xi.
3. Ibid.
4. Ibid., xviii.
5. Ibid., 62.
6. Schlesinger, "Foreword," in O'Connor and Jackson, eds., *American History/American Film*, ix.
7. Ibid., x.
8. Ibid., xvii.
9. Quoted in O'Connor and Jackson, xviii.
10. Rollins, ed., *Hollywood as Historian*, 1.
11. Ibid.
12. Ibid.
13. Leff, "A Test of American Film Censorship," in Rollins, 211.
14. Rosenstone, "History in Images/History in Words," 1174–75.
15. Ibid., 1175.
16. Ibid.
17. Ibid., 1177.
18. Ibid., 1178–79.
19. Ibid., 1180.
20. Ibid., 1181.
21. Ibid., 1184.
22. Toplin, "The Filmmaker as Historian," 1210.

23. Quoted in Toplin, "Filmmaker as Historian," 1213.
24. Ibid.
25. Herlihy, "Am I a Camera?," 1187.
26. Ibid., 1188.
27. Ibid., 1190.
28. Ibid., 1191.
29. White, "Historiography and Historiophoty," 1194.
30. O'Connor, "History in Images/Images in History,"1200.
31. Ibid., 1206.
32. Ibid., 1207.
33. Ibid., 1209.
34. Toplin, *Hollywood as Mirror*, 7.
35. Toplin, "Film Reviews," 1176.
36. Toplin, *Hollywood as Mirror*, ix.
37. Ibid., x.
38. Mintz and Roberts, *Hollywood's America*, ix.
39. Ibid., 247.
40. Rosenstone, *Visions of the Past*, 3.
41. Ibid., 24.
42. Vidal, *Screening History*, 3.
43. Ibid., 39–40.
44. Rossi, "Hitchcock's *Foreign Correspondent*," 26.
45. Ibid., 28.
46. Ibid.
47. Ibid.
48. Jackson, "The Uncertain Peace," 148.
49. Ibid., 162.
50. Ibid., 163.
51. Ibid., 148.

2. TOUGH 'OMBRES AND *BATTLEGROUND*

1. Jones and McClure, *Hollywood at War*.
2. Harry Miller, personal interview, July 23, 1996. All quotations from Miller come from this interview.
3. Monaco, *The Encyclopedia of Film*, 571.
4. Suid, *Guts and Glory*, 76.
5. Ibid.
6. Ibid., 79.
7. Ibid., 80.

8. Kagan, *The War Film*, 85.
9. Hyams, *War Movies*, 114.
10. Jenkins and Hartmann, *Tough 'Ombres!*

3. CARRIERS AND KAMIKAZES:
WING AND A PRAYER

1. James Clayton Hoisington Jr., personal interview, July 1, 1997. Unless otherwise noted, all quotations from Hoisington come from this interview.
2. Maltin, *Leonard Maltin's 1997 Movie and Video Guide*, 1496.
3. "Midway Rethought," *Newsweek*, September 11, 1944, 111.
4. "Lest We Forget," *Commonweal*, September 15, 1944, 518.
5. Basinger, *The World War II Combat Film*, 290.
6. Hoisington, personal communication, June 17, 1997.
7. Ibid.
8. Hoisington, "A History of and by James Clayton Hoisington Jr.," unpublished manuscript (1994), 8.
9. Ibid.
10. Hoisington, personal communication, June 17, 1997.
11. Ibid.
12. Hoisington, "A History," 45.
13. Hoisington, personal communication, June 17, 1997.
14. Hoisington, "A History," 51.
15. Ibid., 48.
16. Ibid.
17. Ibid.
18. Ibid.
19. Ibid.
20. "Lest We Forget," 518.
21. Ibid.
22. Hoisington, personal communication, June 17, 1997.

4. STORMY WEATHER: *MEMPHIS BELLE* AND *TWELVE O'CLOCK HIGH*

1. Jim Oberman, personal interview, January 18, 1997.
2. Andregg, *William Wyler*, 124.
3. *The Memphis Belle*, cowritten and directed by William Wyler, 1944.
4. Doherty, *Projections of War*, 117.

5. Andregg, *William Wyler,* 124.
6. Madsen, *William Wyler*, 238.
7. "The New Pictures: *The Memphis Belle*," 94.
8. *The Memphis Belle.*
9. Andregg, *William Wyler,* 123.
10. "A Terror over Bremen," 75.
11. Ibid.
12. Schickel, "Wheels Up!," 71.
13. "A Terror over Bremen," 75.
14. Lyons, "Tumult in the Clouds," 64.
15. Ibid.
16. Correll, "Real *Twelve O'Clock High*," 70.
17. Ibid.
18. Ibid., 71.
19. Suid, *Guts and Glory*, 80.
20. "New Pictures: *Twelve O'Clock High*," 84.
21. Correll, "Real *Twelve O'Clock High*," 73.
22. "New Pictures: *Twelve O'Clock High*," 84.
23. Butler, *The War Film*, 83.
24. Suid, *Guts and Glory*, 89.

5. *GUADALCANAL DIARY, BACK TO BATAAN,* AND *SANDS OF IWO JIMA:* A VETERAN'S REVIEW

1. Lynn Simpson, personal interview, January 10, 1997. All quotes from Simpson are taken from this interview.
2. Kagan, *The War Film*, 57.
3. Suid, *Guts and Glory*, 39.
4. Quoted in Suid, *Guts and Glory*, 40.
5. The nominations were for Best Supporting Actor (William Bendix), Best Director (John Farrow), Best Original Screenplay (W. R. Burnett and Frank Butler), and Best Picture. *Wake Island* did not win in any of the four categories, but another propaganda film—MGM's *Mrs. Miniver*, about a stalwart British family during the Blitz—was nominated for a dozen Oscars and won six, including Best Picture.
6. Suid, *Guts and Glory*, 48.
7. Kagan, *War Film,* 64.
8. Koppes and Black, *Hollywood Goes to War*, 259.
9. Ibid., 260.
10. Hyams, *War Movies*, 80.

11. Ibid., 97.

12. Ibid.

13. "Before He Returned," 85.

14. "Boston to Bataan," 36.

15. Dick, *The Star-Spangled Screen*, 230.

16. Koppes and Black, *Hollywood Goes to War,* 260–61.

17. Ibid.

18. *Battleground*, discussed in chapter 2, was released the same year, and took advantage of the same added perspective in depicting fighting in the European Theater.

19. Suid, *Guts and Glory,* 95.

20. Ibid.

21. Ibid., 97.

22. Ibid., 98.

23. Ibid.

24. Ibid., 99.

6. STALAG LUFT III: TALES OF
THE GREAT ESCAPE

1. Ernest Thorp, personal interview, March 6, 1997.

2. Brickhill, *The Great Escape*, ix.

3. "The Great Evasion," 80.

4. Ibid., 79.

5. Ibid.

6. Hyams, *War Movies*, 156.

7. Kagan, *The War Film*, 118.

8. "The Getaway," 74.

7. CODE TALKERS, *WINDTALKERS,* AND
TRUE WHISPERS

1. Thomas H. Begay, interview by author. Edwards, IL. September 20, 2008.

2. Smith, "[Review of] *Windtalkers*."

3. "Real Story from a Code Talker."

4. Chinni, "Code Talkers 60 Years Later," 2.

5. Schickel, "*Windtalkers*: Too Breezy."

6. Chinni, "Code Talkers 60 Years Later," 2.

7. Smith, "[Review of] *Windtalkers*."
8. Schickel, "*Windtalkers*: Too Breezy"; "*Windtalkers*: Flat, By-the-book War Movie."
9. "*Windtalkers*: Flat, By-the-book War Movie."
10. Suid, "*Windtalkers* Sends Wrong Message," 2.
11. Ibid., 3.
12. Ibid.
13. Ibid.
14. Ibid., 4.
15. Ninehouse, "True History Is More Interesting," 4.
16. Ibid.
17. Nez quoted in della Cava, "Navajo Code Talkers," 2.
18. Ibid.
19. Doherty, "*Windtalkers*," 36.
20. "He's Like the Wind," 2.
21. Southwell, "Navajos Send a Message," 1.

8. THE ROSIES: LUCY, GOLDIE, GINGER, AND MARGE

1. Marge Mehlberg, personal interview, July 18, 2010.
2. Lucille Broderick, personal interview, August 2, 2012.
3. *The Hidden Army*, 1944.
4. Ibid.
5. Farber, "The Unholy Three," 850.
6. Ibid.
7. *Tender Comrade*, directed by Edward Dmytryk, 1943.
8. Paris, "Lessons for Democracy," xx.
9. *Tender Comrade.*
10. "Current Cinema: *Tender Comrade*," 60.
11. Ibid.
12. Hartung, "While You Are Gone, Dear," 374.
13. Crowther, "*Since You Went Away*."
14. Ibid.
15. "*Since You Went Away*—Box Office/Business," Internet Movie Database, http://www.imdb.com/title/tt0037280/.
16. *Swing Shift*, directed by Jonathan Demme, 1984.
17. *Swing Shift.*
18. *Swing Shift.*
19. Denby, "All Quiet on the Home Front," 87.

20. Ibid.
21. Ebert, *"Swing Shift."*
22. Kessler-Harris, "Rosie the Riveter Goes Hollywood."
23. Davenport, "The Life and Times of Rosie the Riveter," 42–43.
24. Tobias and Anderson, *What Really Happened to Rosie the Riveter?*," 92–97.
25. Kessler-Harris, "Rosie the Riveter Goes Hollywood," 46.
26. Canby, "[Review of] *Swing Shift.*"
27. Paris, "Lessons for Democracy," xx.
28. Paris, "Lessons for Democracy," 85–94.

CONCLUSION

1. Bergman, *We're in the Money.*
2. Biskind, *Seeing Is Believing.*
3. Rosenstone, "History in Images/History in Word."

WORKS CITED

Andregg, Michael A. *William Wyler*. Boston: Twayne Publishers, 1979.

Back to Bataan. Written by Ben Barzman and Richard H. Landau. Directed by Edward Dmytryk. Original release 1945. Turner Home Entertainment DVD.

Basinger, Jeanine. *The World War II Combat Film: Anatomy of a Genre*. New York: Columbia University Press, 1966.

Battleground. Written by Robert Pirosh. Directed by William Wellman. Original release 1949. Warner Home Video DVD.

"Before He Returned." *Newsweek*, July 23, 1945.

Bergman, Andrew. *We're in the Money: Depression America and Its Films*. New York. New York University Press, 1971.

Biskind, Peter. *Seeing Is Believing: How Hollywood Taught Us to Stop Worrying and Love the Fifties*. New York: Pantheon Books, 1983.

"Boston to Bataan." *New Yorker*, September 1, 1945.

Brickhill, Paul. *The Great Escape*. 1950. New York: Norton, 2004.

Butler, Ivan. *The War Film*. South Brunswick, NY: A. S. Barnes and Co., 1974.

Canby, Vincent. "[Review of] *Swing Shift*." *New York Times*, April 13, 1984.

Carnes, Mark C., ed. *Past Imperfect: History According to the Movies*. New York: Holt, 1995.

Chinni, Dante. "Code Talkers 60 Years Later: Sudden Celebrity." *Christian Science Monitor*, July 30, 2002.

Correll, John T. "The Real Twelve O'Clock High." *Air Force Magazine*, January 2011.

Crowther, Bosley. "[Review of] *Since You Went Away*." *New York Times*, July 21, 1944.

"Current Cinema: Tender Comrade." *New Yorker*, June 10, 1944.

Davenport, Sue. "The Life and Times of Rosie the Riveter." *Jump Cut*, April 1983, 42–43.

della Cava, Marco. "Navajo Code Talkers Break 60 Years of Silence." *USA Today*, June 6, 2002.

Denby, David. "All Quiet on the Home Front." *New York*, April 30, 1984.

Dick, Bernard F. *The Star-Spangled Screen: The American World War II Film*. Lexington: University of Kentucky Press, 1985.

Doherty, Thomas. *Projections of War: Hollywood, American Culture, and World War II*, revised edition. New York: Columbia University Press, 2004.

———. "Windtalkers." *Cineaste* 27, no. 4 (2002): 36.

Ebert, Roger. "[Review of] *Swing Shift*." Rogerebert.com. January 1, 1984.http://www.rogerebert.com/reviews /swing-shift-1984.

Farber, Manny. "The Unholy Three." *New Republic*, June 26, 1944.

Gathering of Veterans Friendship Pow Wow, Pamphlet. Seven Circles Heritage Center, Edwards, IL. September 15–17, 2006.

"The Getaway." *Time*, July 17, 1963.

The Great Escape. Written by James Clavell and W. R. Burnett. Directed by John Sturges. Original release 1963. Fox Searchlight DVD.

"The Great Evasion." *Newsweek*, July 15, 1963.

Guadalcanal Diary. Written by Richard Tregaskis and Lamar Trotti. Directed by Lewis Seiler. Original release 1943. 20th Century Fox DVD.

Hartung, Philip T. "While You Are Gone, Dear." *Commonweal*, August 4, 1944.

Herlihy, David. "Am I a Camera? Other Reflections on Film and History." *American Historical Review* 93 (1988): 1186–92.

"He's Like the Wind." *Maclean's*, June 16, 2002.

The Hidden Army. Produced by the United States Army Signal Corps. 1944.

Hoisington, James Clayton, Jr. "A History of and by James Clayton Hoisington, Jr." Unpublished manuscript, 1990.

Hyams, Jay. *War Movies*. New York: Gallery Books, 1984.

Jackson, Martin A. "The Uncertain Peace: The Best Years of Our Lives." In *American History/American Film*, edited by John E. O'Connor and Martin A. Jackson, 147–65. New York: Unger, 1979.

Jenkins, Carl, and Edward George Hartmann. "Tough 'Ombres: The Story of the 90th Infantry Division." Paris: *Stars and Stripes*, 1944. http://www.lonesentry.com/gi_stories_booklets/90thinfantry/.

Jones, Ken D., and Arthur F. McClure. *Hollywood at War: The American Motion Picture and World War II*. New York: Castle Books, 1973.

Kagan, Norman. *The War Film*. New York: Pyramid Publishing, 1974.

Kessler-Harris, Alice. "Rosie the Riveter Goes Hollywood." *Ms.*, July 1984.

Koppes, Clayton R., and Gregory D. Black. *Hollywood Goes to War*. Berkeley and Los Angeles: University of California Press, 1987.

Leff, Leonard J. "A Test of American Film Censorship: Who's Afraid of Virginia Woolf?" In *Hollywood as Historian*, edited by Peter C. Rollins, 211–29. Bowling Green: University of Kentucky Press, 1983.

"Lest We Forget." *Commonweal*, September 15, 1944.

Lyons, Donald. "Tumult in the Clouds." *Film Comment*, November–December 1990.

Madsen, Axel. *William Wyler: Authorized Biography*. New York: Thomas Y. Crowell, 1973.

Maltin, Leonard. *Leonard Maltin's 1997 Movie and Video Guide*. New York: Signet, 1996.

The Memphis Belle. Written by Jerome Chodorov, Lester Koenig, and William Wyler. Directed by William Wyler. Original release 1944. Echo Bridge Home Entertainment DVD.

Memphis Belle. Written by Monte Merrick. Directed by Michael Caton-Jones. Original release 1990. Warner Home Video DVD.

"Midway Rethought." *Newsweek*, September 11, 1944.

Mintz, Steven, and Randy Roberts. eds. *Hollywood's America: United States through Its Films*. St. James, NY: Brandywine, 1993.

Monaco, James. *The Encyclopedia of Film*. New York: Putnam, 1991.

"The New Pictures: *The Memphis Belle*." *Time*, April 17, 1944.

"New Pictures: *Twelve O'clock High*." *Time*, January 30, 1950.

Ninehouse, Everett. "True History Is More Interesting: A New Movie Doesn't Do Justice to the Navajo Code Talkers." *Grand Rapids Press*, June 30, 2002.

O'Connor, John E. "History in Images/Images in History: Reflections on the Importance of Film and Television Study for an Understanding of the Past." *American Historical Review* 93 (1988): 1193–99.

O'Connor, John E., and Martin A. Jackson, eds. *American History/American Film: Interpreting the Hollywood Image*. New York: Unger Press, 1979.

Paris, Michael. "Lessons for Democracy: American Cinema 1942–1945." *European Review of History* 5, no. 1 (1998): 85–94.

Rollins, Peter C., ed. *Hollywood as Historian*. Lexington: University Press of Kentucky, 1983.

Rosenstone, Robert A. "History in Images/History in Word: Reflections on the Possibility of Really Putting History into Film." *American Historical Review* 93 (1988): 1173–85.

———. *Visions of the Past: The Challenge of Film to Our Idea of History*. Cambridge, MA: Harvard University Press, 1995.

Rossi, John. "Hitchcock's Foreign Correspondent (1940)." *Film & History* 12 (1982): 25–32.

Sands of Iwo Jima. Written by Harry Brown and James Edward Grant. Directed by Allan Dwan. Original release 1949. Republic Pictures DVD.

Schickel, Richard. "Wheels Up!" *Time*, October 15, 1990.

———. "*Windtalkers*: Too Breezy." *Time*, June 10, 2002.

Since You Went Away. Written by David O. Selznick. Directed by John Cromwell. Original release 1944. MGM DVD.

Sklar, Robert. *Movie-Made America: A Cultural History of American Movies*. New York: Random House, 1975.

Smith, Neil. "[Review of] *Windtalkers*." BBC.com. August 28, 2002.

Southwell, David. "Navajos Send a Message: World War II Codetalkers Don't Like Film about Them." *Chicago Sun Times*, November 5, 1999.

Suid, Lawrence H. *Guts and Glory: Great American War Films*. Reading, MA: Addison-Wesley, 1978.

———. "*Windtalkers* Sends Wrong Message." *Naval History*, October 2002.

Swing Shift. Written by Nancy Dowd, Bo Goldmand, and Ron Nyswaner. Directed by Jonathan Demme. Original release 1984. Warner Home Video DVD.

Tender Comrade. Written by Dalton Trumbo. Directed by Edward Dmytryk. Original release 1943. Warner Home Video VHS.

"A Terror over Bremen." *Newsweek*, October 22, 1990.

Tobias, Sheila, and Lisa Anderson. *What Really Happened to Rosie the Riveter?: Demobilization and the Female Labor Force, 1944–1947*. New York: MSS Modular Publications, 1974.

Toplin, Robert Brent. "Film Reviews." *Journal of American History* 80, no. 3 (December 1993): 1175.

———. "The Filmmaker as Historian." *American Historical Review* 93 (1988): 1210–27.

———. *Hollywood as Mirror: Changing Views of "Outsiders" and "Enemies" in American Movies*. Westport, CT: Greenwood Press, 1993.

True Whisperers: The Story of the Navajo Code Talkers. Written and directed by Valerie Red-Horse. Original release 2002. PBS DVD.

Twelve O'Clock High. Written by Sy Bartlett and Beirnie Lay Jr. Directed by Henry King. Original release 1949. Fox Searchlight DVD.

Vidal, Gore. *Screening History*. Cambridge, MA: Harvard University Press, 1992.

White, Hayden. "Historiography and Historiophoty." *American Historical Review* 93 (1988): 1193–99.

Windtalkers. Written by John Rice and Joe Batteer. Directed by John Woo. Original release 2002. Fox Searchlight DVD.

"Windtalkers: Flat, By-the-book War Movie." CNN.com, June 14, 2002.

Wing and a Prayer. Written by Jerome Cady. Directed by Henry Hathaway. Original release 1944. 20th Century Fox DVD.

FURTHER READING

GENERAL: THE UNITED STATES IN WORLD WAR II

Adams, Michael C. C. *The Best War Ever*. Baltimore: Johns Hopkins University Press, 1993.

Blum, John Morton. *V Was for Victory: Politics and American Culture during World War II*. New York: Harcourt Brace Jovanovich, 1977.

Kennedy, David M. *The American People in World War II*. New York: Oxford University Press, 2003.

Murray, Williamson, and Allan R. Millett. *A War to Be Won: Fighting the Second World War*. Cambridge, MA: Belknap Press, 2000.

O'Neill, William L. *A Democracy at War: America's Fight at Home and Abroad in World War II*. Cambridge, MA: Harvard University Press, 1995.

Overy, Richard. *Why the Allies Won*. New York: Norton, 1996.

Roeder, George, Jr. *The Censored War: American Visual Experience during World War Two*. New Haven, CT: Yale University Press, 1995.

Takaki, Ronald. *Double Victory: A Multicultural History of America in World War II*. New York: Back Bay Books, 2001.

CHAPTER I

Basinger, Jeanine. *The World War II Combat Film: Anatomy of a Genre*. 1986. Middletown, CT: Wesleyan University Press, 2003.

Birdwell, Michael E. *Celluloid Soldiers: The Warner Bros. Campaign against Nazism*. New York: NYU Press, 2000.

Dick, Bernard F. *The Star-Spangled Screen: The American World War II Film*. Lexington: University Press of Kentucky, 1996.

Doherty, Thomas. *Projections of War: Hollywood, American Culture, and World War II*, revised edition. New York: Columbia University Press, 2004.

Fyne, Robert. *Long Ago and Far Away: Hollywood and the Second World War*. Landham, MD: Scarecrow Press, 2008.

Koppes, Clayton, and Gregory D. Black. *Hollywood Goes to War: How Politics, Profits and Propaganda Shaped World War II Movies*. Berkeley and Los Angeles: University of California Press, 1990.

Rubin, Michael Jay. *Combat Films: American Realism, 1945–2010,* 2nd edition. Jefferson, NC: McFarland, 2011.

Shull, Michael S., and David E. Wilt. *Doing Their Bit: Wartime American Animated Short Films, 1939–1945,* 2nd edition. Jefferson, NC: McFarland, 2004.

CHAPTER 2

Ambrose, Stephen E. *Citizen Soldiers: The U.S. Army from the Normandy Beaches to the Bulge to the Surrender of Germany.* New York: Simon and Schuster, 1997.

———. *Band of Brothers: E Company, 506th Regiment, 101st Airborne from Normandy to Hitler's Eagle's Nest.* New York: Simon and Schuster, 2001.

Atkinson, Rick. *Guns at Last Light: The War in Western Europe, 1944–1945.* New York: Henry Holt, 2013.

Clark, Lloyd. *Crossing the Rhine: Breaking into Nazi Germany 1944 and 1945.* New York: Atlantic Monthly Press, 2008.

Fussell, Paul. *The Boys' Crusade: The American Infantry in Northwestern Europe, 1944–1945.* New York: Modern Library, 2003.

———. *Wartime: Understanding and Behavior in the Second World War.* New York: Oxford University Press, 1989.

Hitchcock, William I. *The Bitter Road to Freedom: The Human Cost of Allied Victory in World War II Europe.* New York: Free Press, 2009.

MacDonald, Charles B. *A Time for Trumpets: The Untold Story of the Battle of the Bulge.* New York: Morrow, 1985.

Toland, John. *Battle: The Story of the Bulge.* 1959. Lincoln, NE: Bison Books, 1999.

CHAPTER 3

Bergerud, Eric M. *Fire in the Sky: The Air War in the South Pacific.* New York: Basic Books, 2001.

Hornfischer, James D. *Neptune's Inferno: The U.S. Navy at Guadalcanal.* New York: Bantam, 2012.

Lundstrom, John B. *The First Team: Pacific Air Combat from Pearl Harbor to Midway.* Annapolis, MD: Naval Institute Press, 2005.

Moore, Stephen L. *Pacific Payback: The Carrier Aviators Who Avenged Pearl Harbor at the Battle of Midway.* New York: NAL Hardcover, 2014.

Parshall, Jonathan, and Anthony Tully. *Shattered Sword: The Untold Story of the Battle of Midway.* Washington, DC: Potomac Books, 2007.

Spector, Ronald. *Eagle against the Sun: The American War against Japan.* New York: Vintage, 1985.

Thomas, Evan. *Sea of Thunder: Four Commanders and the Last Great Naval Campaign, 1941–1945.* New York: Simon and Schuster, 2006.

Toll, Ian W. *Pacific Crucible: War at Sea in the Pacific, 1941–1942.* New York: Norton, 2012.

White, Bill, and Robert Gandt. *Intrepid: The Epic Story of America's Most Legendary Warship.* New York: Broadway Books, 2008.

CHAPTER 4

Astor, Gerald. *The Mighty Eighth: The Air War in Europe as Told by the Men Who Fought It.* New York: Dutton, 1997.

Ayres, Travis L. *Bomber Boys: The Heroes Who Flew the B-17s in World War II.* New York: Berkeley/Caliber, 2005.

Caidin, Martin. *Flying Forts: The B 17 in World War II.* New York: Meredith Books, 1968.

Miller, Donald L. *Masters of the Air: America's Bomber Boys Who Fought the Air War against Nazi Germany.* New York: Simon and Schuster, 2006.

O'Neill, Brian. *Half a Wing, Three Engines, and a Prayer: B-17s over Germany.* New York: McGraw-Hill Professional, 1999.

Overy, Richard. *The Bombers and the Bombed: Allied Air War over Europe, 1940–1945.* New York: Viking, 2014.

Schaffer, Ronald B. *Wings of Judgment: American Bombing in World War II.* New York: Oxford University Press, 1988.

Werrell, Kenneth P. *Death from the Heavens: A History of Strategic Bombing.* Annapolis, MD: Naval Institute Press, 2009.

CHAPTER 5

Bergerud, Eric. M. *Touched with Fire: The Land War in the South Pacific.* New York: Penguin, 1997.

Breuer, William B. *Retaking the Philippines: Return to Bataan and Corregidor, 1944–1945.* New York: St. Martin's, 1986.

Frank, Richard B. *Guadalcanal: The Definitive Account of the Landmark Battle.* New York: Penguin, 1992.

Leckie, Robert. *Helmet for My Pillow: From Parris Island to the Pacific.* 1957. New York: Bantam Books, 2010.

Prados, John. *Islands of Destiny: The Solomons Campaign and the Eclipse of the Rising Sun.* New York: New American Library, 2012.

Sledge, E. B. *With the Old Breed: At Peleliu and Okinawa.* 1981. New York: Presidio Press, 2007.

Spector, Ronald. *Eagle against the Sun: The American War against Japan.* New York: Vintage, 1985.

Tregaski, Richard. *Guadalcanal Diary.* 1942. New York: Modern Library, 2000.

Wukovits, John. *One Square Mile of Hell: The Battle for Tarawa.* New York: New American Library, 2007.

CHAPTER 6

Brickhill, Paul. *The Great Escape.* 1951. New York: Norton, 2004.

Carroll, Tim. *The Great Escape from Stalag Luft III: The Full Story of How 76 Allied Officers Carried Out World War II's Most Remarkable Mass Escape.* New York: Gallery Books, 2005.

Clark, A. P. *33 Months as a POW in Stalag Luft III: A World War II Airman Tells His Story.* Golden, CO: Fulcrum Books, 2005.

Durand, Arthur A. *Stalag Luft III: The Secret Story.* Baton Rouge: Louisiana State University Press, 1988.

Pearson, Simon. *The Great Escaper: The Life and Death of Roger Bushell—Love, Betrayal, Big X and the Great Escape.* London: Hodder and Stoughton, 2013.

Read, Simon. *The Human Game: The True Story of the "Great Escape" Murders and the Hunt for the Gestapo Gunmen.* New York: Berkeley, 2012.
Sage, Jerry. *Sage.* New York: Dell, 1985.

CHAPTER 7

Bernstein, Alison R. *American Indians and World War II: Toward a New Era in Indian Affairs.* Norman: University of Oklahoma Press, 1999.
Child, Brenda J. *Boarding School Seasons: American Indian Families, 1900–1940.* Lincoln: University of Nebraska Press, 2000.
Gilbert, Ed. *Native American Code Talkers in World War II.* Oxford: Osprey, 2012.
Mack, Stephen. *It Had to Be Done: The Navajo Code Talkers Remember World War II.* Tucson, AZ: Whispering Dove Design, 2008.
Nez, Chester, and Judith Schiess Avila. *Code Talker: The First and Only Memoir by One of the Original Navajo Code Talkers of WWII.* New York: Berkeley, 2012.
Paul, Doris A. *The Navajo Code Talkers.* 1973. Pittsburgh, PA: Dorrance Publishing, 1998.

CHAPTER 8

Gluck, Sherna Burger. *Rosie the Riveter Revisited: Women, the War, and Social Change.* Boston: Twayne, 1987.
Kiernan, Denise. *The Girls of Atomic City: The Untold Story of the Women Who Helped Win World War II.* New York: Touchstone, 2014.
Knaff, Donna B. *Beyond Rosie the Riveter: Women of World War II in American Popular Graphic Art.* Lawrence: University Press of Kansas, 2013.
Litoff, Judith Barrett, and David C. Smith, eds. *Since You Went Away: World War II Letters from American Women on the Home Front.* Lawrence: University of Kansas Press, 1995.
Reid, Constance Bowman. *Slacks and Calluses: Our Summer in a Bomber Factory.* Washington, DC: Smithsonian Books, 2000.
Yellin, Emily. *Our Mothers' War: American Women at Home and at the Front during World War II.* New York: Free Press, 2005.

INDEX

ABOUT THE AUTHOR

Suzanne Broderick teaches history at Illinois State University, where she developed an interdisciplinary course entitled *Hollywood History* that allowed her to marry her two great interests: Hollywood film and American history. Her fascination with war films began as a very young child, when she attended the local cinemas in her small hometown during the late 1950s and 1960s.